Gardening Together

A month-by-month guide
to getting the most from
your outdoor space

Diarmuid Gavin
& Paul Smyth

GILL BOOKS

Gill Books
Hume Avenue
Park West
Dublin 12
www.gillbooks.ie

Gill Books is an imprint of M.H. Gill and Co.

© Diarmuid Gavin and Paul Smyth 2022

9780717192526

Designed by Graham Thew
Edited by Jane Rogers
Indexed by Eileen O'Neill

For permission to reproduce photographs, the authors
and publisher gratefully acknowledge the following:

© Mark Nixon: iv, ix, 9; Author advice features
© Ruth Medjber.

Printed by Printer Trento, Italy
This book is typeset in 11pt on 14pt Freight Text Pro

A CIP catalogue record for this book is available from
the British Library.

5 4 3 2 1

MIX
Paper | Supporting
responsible forestry
FSC® C015829

To Justine

Contents

Introduction

Hello! Welcome to our book, *Gardening Together*.
First, a brief introduction. We are Diarmuid Gavin, garden designer, TV presenter and podcaster, and Paul Smyth, plantsman, propagator and ... podcaster!

We're both from Ireland and we've worked on this island and in many other places around the globe. We love plants, we're interested in how they grow, and we love using collections of them to create gardens. A few years ago we started working together, planting gardens and broadcasting over Instagram. And those connections have led to our podcast, *Dirt*, and now this, a book based on many garden conversations we've enjoyed through the changing seasons.

Gardening is changing. More people than ever before are interested in gardening, so follow us on our garden-year journey from January to December. We take a month-by-month look at gardens and aim to provide some simple tips and tricks you can use to create your dream garden. Whether you're brand new to gardening or a dab hand at the potting bench, we hope to inspire, delight and inform you so that you will get the most out of your space all year round.

Diarmuid's story

We made the big move from London to Wicklow 13 years ago. Eppie, my daughter, was just two, and the house we chose was a new-build nestled in an idyllic location at the foot of the Sugarloaf but still just 35 minutes from the airport.

Our garden consisted of a third of an acre of builder-laid sloped lawn looking out to a field beyond. I'd find out soon enough that the ground was a challenge to dig, but for the first few years I did very little. Designing my own garden proved to be an unexpected challenge. I knew what I wanted – to tame the slope by introducing terraces, to grow a lush green Wicklow jungle using architectural plants such as the tree fern (*Dicksonia antarctica*), bananas, cannas and bamboo. I also planned to grow some fruit trees and have an area for vegetables, and I wanted to build a pond. I wanted to live up to the principles of design I'd always believed in – which is to blur the lines between home and garden.

The house was a big bland box, with small windows to the rear, from which there was a great view of trees, fields and mountains. I needed to find a way of bursting through the pebbledash and opening it to the garden. The dream was to be able to wander from each room upstairs onto a wide balcony or veranda under the cover of an overhanging roof and use the upstairs space as an outdoor room.

The dream had to wait while reality kicked in. There were other priorities – swings and a trampoline, and open space for exuberant puppies. And I'd emptied the bank buying the house, so the garden would have to evolve slowly.

The realities of the plot were also sinking in. Building the house had led to severe soil compaction. A meagre amount of topsoil had been spread over this compacted soil, and once I began to dig I unearthed a small quarry's worth of shale and boulders. My dream garden would take some time to realise, and a lot of back-breaking work would be required. Time turned out to be a blessing, though, as living with the space for a couple of years led to my imagination kicking in. And time allowed me relax into the search for the structures I needed to start work.

Eventually I found what I was looking for: nine hundred-year-old cast-iron columns lying in a city architectural salvage yard. They were marked as having been made in Bristol in 1895 and were formerly used to support part of a city-centre hospital. They could now support the framework for a second-level terrace and roof, meaning that I could have a wide second-level veranda. This notion had been inspired by my travels, especially trips to New Zealand, South Africa, Florida's Key West and Venice Beach in California. Outdoor living has been key to architectural development in these countries and I believe it should also be in ours.

My breakthrough moment came in Charleston, South Carolina. I was filming at a colonial ranch where the movie *The Notebook* had been made, and in the city I hired a bicycle and came across the area's iconic 'single' houses – long, narrow homes with piazzas that stretch down the entire side. This distinctive house style was shaped by the city's hot and humid summers and the homes are oriented specifically to take advantage of cooling breezes.

Wicklow offered a more pleasant climate, and there was less of a requirement for cooling air, but the protection of a protruding roof would make a useful umbrella from our regular rain, which arrives as gentle droplets or torrential downpours. A covered veranda would also allow an unusual view over the garden and let me indulge in my love for tree ferns – as viewed from above!

There were missteps. My first deadline was to have the veranda up and the garden tamed in time for Eppie's holy communion party. I was garden gallivanting abroad and the contractor chosen to install lawns, terraces and ponds proved to be a disaster. While the garden looked good, underneath the newly laid turf the soil had once again been heavily compacted with machinery; sand rather than topsoil had been used as a bed for the lawns; and the ponds leaked! I would spend years undoing the damage.

More time passed and eventually, just five years ago, I began to get serious about the plot and started planting in earnest.

Saturdays were spent in garden centres and nurseries. My penchant was always for trees first – we've squeezed in about 60 – and then broad-leaved architectural species: the lusted-after giant ferns, cannas, *Musa*, cordylines and ornamental gingers.

Suddenly, after eight 'nothing' years, it seemed we had the beginnings of a jungle. Renowned gardener Helen Dillon came for Sunday lunch and brought a beautiful magnolia, 'Leonard Messel', which has pride of place in the collection; and I found a gorgeous tetrapanax at Architectural Plants. Other leftover plants from projects were fitted in, like the conical bay trees that had once revolved at the Chelsea Flower Show and that now form evergreen pillars in this Wicklow plot. There's even a sequoia and a monkey puzzle, so in a few years decisions will have to be made about what stays. That's the fun of planting a garden.

The real revelation was *Geranium palmatum* happily self-seeding under the tree ferns and producing a haze of pink froth from late April through to mid-July. We had to pinch ourselves. We were at last developing a garden we loved. There were garden arguments along the way – I wanted less lawn and more plants, so the grass was gradually consumed. And I'd no sooner start on a project than I'd dream up another. These projects were becoming like painting the Forth Bridge; it's such an involved and time-consuming process of improvement that it never truly ends. And this was at odds with my lifestyle. I worked abroad so I'd arrive home around 11.30 on a Friday night and, first thing on

Saturday morning, wander into the garden, bleary-eyed and barefoot, dogs yapping at my ankles. I'd look for what had happened while I was away – what was growing, budding, flowering? What wasn't? What needed doing? My plot eyed me back suspiciously; it was fine, thank you ... no need of your help ... we're all doing okay without you. Then, after a mug of strong coffee, and armed with spade, secateurs or shears, I'd fight my way in. And at 11 p.m. I'd emerge, exhausted and delighted, and with even more ideas. And I'd do it all over again on Sunday.

And in January 2020 I resolved to take things further. Paul Smyth came round and built some compost heaps, I hired a digger, the last of the lawns went and half the garden was once again a mess waiting for another year of weekends. Paul had begun to work with me a few years ago after four years at the world-famous Crûg Farm nursery in North Wales. He had great plant knowledge and was good with a spade.

And then came Covid-19. Like everyone else, I was isolated at home from mid-March, with nothing to do but garden. On 18 March I met Paul at a motorway service station. We were planning more work in my plot and for a garden at the 2021 Chelsea show. But things were different. There was no shaking of hands and no seats or tables in use, so we chatted over the bonnet of my car. A few hours later, back at home, I called Paul. The weather was great and there was something we could do during this lockdown period. Over the past few years the picture-sharing app Instagram had become an inspiration. Gardeners from everywhere shared photos, videos and information about plants and their plots and chatted to each other.

And so 'Garden Conversations' started that evening; a daily 7 p.m. broadcast from my home design studio and Paul's Carlow potting shed. We'd play records on vinyl, drink coffee and have the craic. It was like pirate radio for green-fingered geeks. Each evening I popped an iPad on the desk and called Paul or other gardening friends – Rory in Galway, Darragh in Rathfarnham, Mark in London. Their faces would pop up on the screen and an audience began to build. In the tens at first, then hundreds, and then by the thousand. We undertook masterclasses on design, planting and the crafts of gardening. Our audience became a tribe, gathering each evening, chatting, laughing, joking, learning and slagging.

We answered thousands of questions, played our music, called up gardeners from around the globe. We had competitions: gardening quizzes that were impossible to win, and a contest for best floral hat, judged by Paul Costelloe, which brought tons of entries.

Soon gifts started to arrive at my house – chocolates, cakes and even record collections. A community was building of people who liked plants and gardens and who appreciated having an hour of each day to escape.

The broadcast has now moved on to an irreverent weekly gardening podcast called *Dirt* and we hope *Gardening Together* becomes a companion to that.

Paul's story

Gardening and propagation wasn't exactly a calling from birth, but something that has evolved over time into a major interest. I grew up on the family farm in Carlow in rural south-east Ireland, and veg-growing was my first passion – it's a great introduction to gardening, a fantastic way both to learn and build confidence in propagation.

I studied at Waterford Institute of Technology. On the first day I only wanted to know how to grow veg; but by the end of the three years, and having been immersed in plant identification, husbandry and propagation, I had a very different outlook.

I spent a year working for Irish landscape architect and gardener Angela Jupe in her garden, Bellefield. There, my interest in plants escalated, as did my fascination with propagation. On one of my last days there Angela mentioned twin-scaling – it's a propagation method for bulbs. (It basically takes advantage of a bulb's defence mechanism, which kicks in when they are damaged. In fact, a lot of propagation uses this basic principle.) I was intrigued, and the conversation led to me doing two research projects as part of my degree.

I left Ireland for Evolution Plants in Wiltshire to work on a giant snowdrop collection, of all things! It was my responsibility to record, organise and then propagate, ready to launch a snowdrop mail order nursery. I spent months indoors chopping up bulbs in a semi-sterile environment, creating 50,000 snowdrops.

On a rare day off I went to the Grow London show in Battersea Park and came face to face with Sue from the renowned Crûg Farm nursery. I soon found myself on a dark bank-holiday Monday evening wending my way along the A5 and into the heart of Snowdonia to join their team. As the landscape got wilder and the houses fewer I asked myself what on earth I was doing.

My time at Crûg was definitely when my plant knowledge was tested, honed and vastly improved. I started as the gardener and progressed eventually to propagator, and within a year I was giving tours, listing off unpronounceable plant names to equally perplexed visitors. The collection of plants at Crûg is incredible and the variety impressive. When I took over the propagating job, the responsibility of the potted stock came with it, as did the realisation of the complexities of managing such a unique collection. The most exciting (and equally terrifying) part was the challenge of propagating this collection, many of which weren't in cultivation – quite often when I consulted propagation manuals the plant name wasn't listed and, in some rare instances, neither was the family!

Back to basics is the answer in this case. Observing growth habits, type of growth and timing are all important. As is experimentation and just taking a chance.

In some cases this is easily done, but you are often faced with a plant that yields one cutting a year, so an educated guess needs to be well calculated. But that, for me, is the joy of propagation. The experimentation aspect and the thrill of cracking a particularly hard plant is what keeps me going. I was known to occasionally (when something went particularly right) run excitedly into Crûg's office with the rooted or germinated plant in hand.

When you hold in your hand the largest known population of a particular plant outside its native habitat, it humbles you, but it also reminds you of the importance of plant propagation and the skill that you are mastering, as well as the importance of getting that information into the public domain so that everyone can benefit from it, particularly the people in the country where the material originated from. My favourite part of the job was talking to other propagators, sharing tips and solving problems.

Since leaving Crûg to work with Diarmuid I've missed the experimentation and the challenges, but my new role has allowed me to use plants in gardens, following them to maturity, not just focusing on producing them. My own gardening style is what I like to describe as benign neglect, though others might call it negligence. Either way, it means that what I grow is reliable and tough. I'm a believer in leaving plants to their own devices and not getting too worried about weeds.

I've been fortunate enough to garden in a few different places, primarily in my parents' garden in County Carlow, where the snowdrops steal the winter show and the cottage-garden plants spill onto the paths in the summer.

In North Wales, on the periphery of Snowdonia National Park, where I lived and gardened for a few years, I have a steep garden at the back of a miner's cottage. It too is stuffed with plants mostly left to their own devices.

Plants are my thing. I'm fascinated by how and why they grow, what they do, how they look and how we can grow them in our gardens. Picking a favourite is impossible, so through the course of this book I've picked a favourite plant for each month, some more ordinary, others some of the most extraordinary plants I've come across. All can be grown on these islands, and all will inject a little magic into your garden in that particular month.

When faced with that initial trip to a garden centre the best advice I can offer is to always be prepared and take a list. Even if you don't stick entirely to your list, it will remind you what you can buy and what you need. And you'll always come back with more than you bargained for. That's one of the many joys of gardening ... depending on whom you ask!

I've been lucky enough to do a job I love, and in this book I hope to share some of what I've learned. Gardening is a profession that's as much about the process as the end result. I love the seasons and the fresh start every new year brings. This book sets out what to do on a month-by-month basis, picking relevant topics each month to hopefully inspire you to get out into the garden.

January

January is a shitshow. Christmas is over and there's a dearth of joy. Daylight hours are in short supply and there is really very little appealing in the garden. If you go out and take a look you might find a few beauties making themselves seen or creating a scent in your plot; but if you actually attempt to do anything in the garden this month you can do more harm than good. The garden is best viewed from a window. So, book an Airbnb in Florida, eat fries and watch movies.

Opposite: *Helleborus argutifolius* with a winter sprinkling of frost.

January is, however, a great month to consider planting – and maybe to plant. Provided the weather plays ball, almost any type of plant and style of planting scheme can be planted.

Weather is important because of the effect it has on our soil. If it's a wet winter the ground can be waterlogged. If it's extremely cold the soil may be frozen or covered in snow. Cold weather, including frost and lingering snow, can cause the water in plant cells to freeze, which damages the cell walls. Frost-damaged plants may become limp, blackened and distorted. Some leaves that are suffering from frost damage take on a translucent appearance. Frost in the soil has a more serious effect on plant roots. Prolonged periods of extreme cold can restrict the ability of roots to take up moisture and the plant may die. So be careful. But if the soil turns easily, and the temperature is above freezing, it's a great time to plant.

Above left: Winter shot of Diarmuid's garden.
Left: Rhododendron covered in snow.
Opposite: Frost on *Lonicera nitida* leaves.

Planting a garden

We're going to look at different types of plants for each month of the year, kicking off with the most important group – trees.

All plants breathe life into a garden and every level of planting has a role to play: perennials for colour, contrast and filling the spaces in the soil; shrubs to create boundaries and structure, to mask unsightly things and to frame others; and trees to add the final dimension – to draw the outline, to create cover and add focal points like nothing else can do.

Trees provide a huge number of benefits to your individual ecosystem and to our wider one. They are aesthetically beautiful, they remove and store carbon from the atmosphere, they reduce the risk of flooding through slowing the effects of heavy rain, and their roots bind soil together, reducing the occurrence of soil erosion. The physical weight of a tree consists of approximately 50 per cent carbon and they enhance our air quality enormously by absorbing pollutants through their leaves and trapping and filtering contaminants in the air. They also produce oxygen through photosynthesis.

When planning a plot it's important to make the best possible choice of trees. Choose a type or a group that will grow happily in your garden's natural conditions and within the available space. Take a look at your garden and imagine the journey through the space. Begin to consider where trees should go, what type they should be, what roles they will play. Think about which trees you love. As part of an overall plan trees may be punctuation points, beautiful forms that lead your journey, indicating where to stop and rest and signposting where to look next. They may be the guardians that enclose the space or the shining stars that create the main interest.

Before acquiring a tree, research the options you're considering. Explore your site and your soil and select something that you know will mature into a great specimen. You need to know the eventual height and spread of a tree before you plant it, even more so if you intend to position it in your front garden or near the house. You have a responsibility to ensure that the tree will not become a danger to the general public (branches could fall on passers-by or even onto the road), that it will not start to undermine the foundations of the house and that it won't take over your garden.

Small to medium-sized gardens

Always find out from the nursery, garden centre or label what the eventual height and spread of the tree will be. If there's no space in your plot for spreading branches, there are plenty of fastigiate or columnar trees – these are tall, slim beanpoles that will reach for the sky and not your boundaries.

Similarly, if you don't want a tree that's going to dominate through its height, there are many beautiful low-growing trees to choose from. So whether you are vertically or horizontally challenged, need a specimen in a lawn or something nice for a pot on a balcony, there are lots of interesting choices available. Here are our favourite trees for small to medium-sized gardens.

Cercis canadensis 'Forest Pansy'

The eastern redbud is native to North America and the state tree of Oklahoma. Gorgeous magenta pink flowers open in great profusion on bare stems in spring, followed by wonderful heart-shaped leaves in reddish, purplish-wine colours, and then by a colourful autumnal display. Its eventual height will be about 7.5 metres. Plant as a stand-alone specimen to be admired.

Right: Blooms of *Cercis*.

Styrax japonicus (Japanese snowbell)

Laden with very pretty, fragrant white bell-shaped flowers in spring, this is a tree whose show is best admired from underneath, so, for example, a bench placed underneath the tree would make an ideal viewing spot in the early summer. Prefers a sheltered spot. Eventual height and spread around 7.5 metres.

Liquidambar

Liquidambar, or sweetgum, is a majestic tree, reaching in maturity over 20 metres in height. It produces one of the best autumnal displays, with its five lobed leaves, a bit like a maple, that turn purple, crimson and burgundy. If you love this tree but, like most of us, don't have the space to grow it, an alternative is 'Gumball'. This is a dwarf, shrubby version of the tree – it is also sometimes grafted onto a standard stem to create a lollipop shape. It will grow to around 3 metres in height over time, with a compact rounded head.

Arbutus unedo (strawberry tree)

Arbutus unedo is a beautiful small evergreen tree with much to recommend it all year round – glossy green leaves, a light, luxuriously mahogany-coloured bark, small white urn-shaped flowers and a strawberry-like fruit. As the fruit are formed from last year's flowers, you will often find them and the flowers at the same time, which is highly unusual. Combined with an interesting growth habit, this tree makes a great specimen and grows well in both dry and heavy clay soils, and it tolerates pollution, so it thrives in the city. For extra bijou gardens, there is a dwarf version – 'Compacta'.

Cornus controversa 'Variegata' (wedding-cake tree)

This is a lovely 'centre of the lawn' tree. Branches grow in a layered fashion, similar to the tiers of a wedding cake, giving rise to its common name. Leaves are green with creamy-white margins, turning yellow in the autumn.

Ornamental cherry

The tall, slim *Prunus* 'Amanagowa' grows no wider than 2.5m and usually no taller than 6m. Cheal's weeping cherry (*Prunus* 'Kiku-shidare-zakura') grows to around 3 metres and is covered in double pink flowers come April and May. These Fuji cherries are suitable for container growing and small spaces and are the epitome of Japanese delicacy with soft early spring blooms and a blaze of autumnal foliage colour. For a dazzling flourish of brilliant colour to cheer you up in February, choose the flowering apricot *Prunus mume* 'Beni-chidori'. This has deliciously almond-scented deep pink blossoms on bare stems. Paul's choice is *Prunus incisa* 'Kojo-no-mai'. While more a shrub than a tree, it has all the beauty of ornamental cherries but reaches no more than 2.5 metres in height. Slow growing, but worth the wait.

Cornus kousa 'Miss Satomi'

Cornus kousa 'Miss Satomi' is a good choice if you have room for a tree to spread laterally but you just don't want it to grow tall. Most of us are familiar with the colourful stems of dogwood (**Cornus**) in winter, but 'Miss Satomi' is better known for her deep pink flowers. The branches are outstretched and the leaves turn purple and deep red in autumn. It could also be fan trained against a wall, which is a good way of incorporating trees and shrubs into small spaces.

Acacia dealbata (mimosa)

Acacia dealbata, also known as mimosa, has beautiful silvery fern-like foliage that flower arrangers love and is covered in January with yellow pom-pom flowers that have the most delicious fragrance. It can be slightly tender, especially when young, although it seems to get hardier with age.

Azara microphylla

The flowers of this tree have a gorgeous vanilla scent from tiny greenish-yellow flowers produced in late winter and early spring. It's a small evergreen shrub or tree with small dark-green leaves and will tolerate some shade.

Pyrus salicifolia 'Pendula' (weeping pear)

The weeping pear is a pendulous small tee with soft mint-green leaves. It's a really pretty tree that makes an elegant focal point in the centre of a lawn or gravel area where it can be admired.

Crataegus laevigata 'Paul's Scarlet'

A compact hawthorn that is covered in crimson flowers in the late spring and early summer. A great tree if your garden is less sheltered. And it's called Paul!

Opposite: Cherry tree in full blossom.

Above: *Crataegus laevigata* 'Paul's Scarlet'.

Acer griseum (paper bark maple)

You'll never tire of the wonderful coppery peeling bark of this maple. In addition, it puts on a good autumn display of red and orange. It's a medium-sized tree, but slow growing, so it won't take over anytime soon. Like lots of acers, it does best in a garden with shelter from the coldest winds:

Malus 'Evereste'

Crab apples make fantastic trees for a small garden. They can easily tamed be and aren't huge even when they reach full maturity. They are covered in a profusion of blossom in spring and followed in the autumn and early winter by the most amazing fruits that look like Christmas baubles. 'Evereste' has red, flushed-orange to yellow fruits in winter and keeps a conical shape. Very adaptable to windy sites too.

Topiary

Shrubs and trees which can be tightly clipped into topiary shapes are always good candidates for the small garden. Laurel, bay, yew, holly, *Lonicera nitida* and privet can all be transformed into neat lollipops, pyramids or other shapes and kept to size with a regular pruning regime. They are best suited to a formal-style garden and work well in front gardens.

Opposite: Crab apple in midwinter.
This page: Examples of different types of topiary in London nurseries and gardens.

Beautiful tree bark

DIARMUID

The bark of a tree often looks its best when its dressing of leaves has fallen away. Many deciduous specimens show off their bark armour in January. Outside the garden, in bogs or on hills, I love to observe the beauty of a self-seeded tree, with bark bared and stems shaped and pruned by the wind.

While we're in January, let's take a moment to consider bark. Winter reveals all – it takes away the drapes and the clothing and it shows that if considered choices have been made at the time of planting, a tree's bark can be as enticing and entertaining as its foliage or flowers.

Betula utilis var. *Jacquemontii* or the Himalayan white birch has the most brilliant white bark that shines in the winter; there are other specimens whose barks are outstanding too.

Prunus serrula, the Tibetan cherry tree, has a glossy coppery brown bark that is revealed when the old bark has peeled off – so shiny you want to reach out and touch it.

Another wonderful species is *Acer griseum*, known as the paperbark because its chestnut-coloured bark flakes away gradually like sheets of paper to reveal a stunning deep orange to red bark underneath.

The Cyprus strawberry tree, *Arbutus × andranchnoides*, also has peeling bark in cinnamon red colours.

Sometimes it is the twisted silhouette of a bare stem that draws the eye – corkscrew willow (*Salix matsudana* 'Tortuosa') and twisted hazel (*Corylus avellana* 'Contorta') are both beloved of florists for their spiralling, curling stems.

The red dogwood (*Cornus stolonifera*) and yellow-stemmed cornus don't draw much attention to themselves during the year, but following their annual striptease they will add vibrant colour to the winter garden.

Opposite: *Acer palmatum* 'Bloodgood'.
Over: Natural bonsai in Snowdonia.

Top tips for planting bare-root trees in January

1

Buy your trees as young as possible; they will adapt quickly to your situation.

2

Don't let roots dry out. Have some damp hessian nearby to keep them covered.

3

Have some compost and slow-release fertilizer at hand to give the trees a strong start.

4

Plant to where there is a soil mark on the stem – not higher, not lower.

5

This can be a windy time of the year, so use a stake and tree ties. Put the stake in the planting hole before you plant the tree so that you do not pierce the roots.

6

Choose tree ties that are expandable, so they don't strangle the tree. Loosen these ties as the tree grows. Check them every six months. You should be able to remove them in two years.

7

Plant singly or in groups, depending on what you are trying to achieve.

8

Don't plant in extreme frost because the soil can crack and lift, exposing the roots. You want your trees comfortably bedded in for spring growth.

Opposite: Paul's garden in the winter light.

Boundaries

Garden boundaries are often an integral part of the overall design of a garden. They help to define your space and provide a backdrop and background colour to the planting. They can give shelter and help create microclimates, enabling you to cultivate more tender species.

It may be that you are fortunate to have inherited beautifully kept hedges or a period wall to start from, but you may find yourself having to start from scratch with broken-down wooden fences and scrappy overgrown hedges. Consider all options carefully before making decisions on what to build or plant. A hedge will take time to establish, and a brick wall will be a costly choice if you change your mind.

Our preference, and by far the most environmentally friendly option, is almost always a hedge, formal or informal. We're spoilt for choice – there are tons of options available. Consider what's important for you – evergreen, good autumn foliage, flowers, berries. And think about the ultimate size you require. There can be substantial differences in growth rates and eventual heights, so gather all the facts before you make your choice.

A gentle warning: there have been many neighbourhood disputes reported in the press about leylandii hedges growing out of control, blocking out the light and destroying surrounding gardens. This type of hedge is best restricted to larger park areas because, unless well maintained, they outgrow most residential sites.

As well as the overall aesthetic value, consider privacy requirements, security and, if you are near a busy road, noise pollution. A planted boundary at the appropriate height will help to cut out noise. How much maintenance are you prepared to do? An informal hedge may require only an annual trim, but a formal hedge will need clipping two or three times in the growing season to keep it looking great.

Opposite: A different boundary: an espaliered cedar tree.

What hedge to choose

Evergreen hedges

Candidates for great evergreen hedges include yew, box, holly, escallonia, euonymus, osmanthus, Portuguese laurel and photinia.

Yew and box are slow growing and some gardeners are shying away from *Buxus* because of the fear of box blight. *Lonicera nitida*, *Ilex crenata* or some of the smaller-leaved hebes can make good alternatives.

Photinia and laurel can grow to a good height more quickly and provide a glossy foil; the laurel bears small white flowers in June, and the photinia has distinctive young foliage in reddish bronze.

Viburnum tinus is an evergreen shrub that produces clusters of pink buds that open into scented white flowers late in the year. If trimmed regularly it makes an elegant hedge.

Deciduous hedges

Deciduous plants can offer more flowering opportunities for hedging. Consider scented *Viburnum farreri*, roses like *Rosa* 'Roseraie de l'Hay', spiraea and weigelas.

Classic deciduous choices are beech, which hangs on to its coppery autumn foliage through winter; hawthorn, which is an excellent choice for a wildlife corridor; and hornbeam.

Deciduous hedges are best planted in the dormant season, from leaf fall in November through to early February.

Bamboo

Bamboos create soft but definite garden boundaries. With many species to choose from, the most important consideration is how much space you have and how invasive the individual bamboo is – choose clump-forming varieties that won't invade your neighbour's plot.

Bamboo canes are available in green, black and golden yellow. They have varying eventual heights and different leaf proportions give each plant a very different feel. They rustle in the wind and create a wonderful feeling in the garden. They won't thrive in dry situations – they are thirsty plants and love water.

Walls and fences

Walls may have a place. They can be constructed in areas that have an inhospitable growing climate. They can smarten up a garden, creating an air of formality and a definite sense of style. But, again, consider the options carefully. Look at the colour and texture of your house and its locality and match the materials as closely as possible.

Reclaimed brick and stone is widely available and is worth the extra investment as it will truly unify the space. If you require formality, but still need some green, the combination of low brick walls with a neatly clipped hedge behind or on top can be elegant. It can also help hide the bottom of the hedge.

A wall in bad condition can be rendered to give it a new lease of life; rendered walls will look great in most styles of garden and the paint colour can be matched with the house or other hard landscaping in the garden.

Wooden boundaries have really moved on since the classic upright timber fence. Wooden walls constructed with solid horizontal decking can finish the look of a house and garden beautifully and they last much longer than the traditional fence. They have strong architectural value and offer a greater sense of security.

Paul's plant of the month

The corkscrew hazel *Corylus avellana* 'Contorta' is a great tough plant that thrives on the windy hillside of my garden but would do equally well in a small suburban plot. Easily sourced and easy to grow, its leaves aren't to everyone's taste in the summer, but I grow mine among buddleias and shrub roses, so it goes unnoticed in the main season, but once the other plants are pruned in early winter its weird and wonderful twisted stems really stand out.

In the January garden

When trees are stripped of their leaves, when bulbs are still hiding, when our herbaceous perennials don't dare to peep their heads out from under their compost and soil blankets, the plants that are performing shine like jewels in otherwise dormant plots.

There are delightful rewards for searching for these jewels, so let's have a January wander through the garden and see what we find.

Wintersweet, or *Chimonanthus praecox*, is a midwinter treasure, its pale-yellow waxy-looking flowers on bare stems emitting a delicious scent. It's best grown against a warm south-facing wall.

For easy-to-grow fragrance, try *Viburnum farreri*, which never disappoints. Its white flowers, tinged with pink, have an exquisite bouquet; they're also borne on bare stems.

It's not just scent we're looking for, though – when foliage drops, it can reveal hitherto hidden beauty. Dogwood shrubs come into their own in winter. Fully clothed, they are unremarkable, but when their bare stems are revealed, you can appreciate the vivid colour of their stems. *Cornus alba* 'Sibirica' is the bright-red one, and *Cornus sericea* 'Flaviramea' has yellow-green stems.

Opposite: Frost on flowers of *Chaenomeles japonica* (Japanese quince).

Hardwood cuttings

One of the easiest ways to produce new plants is by taking hardwood cuttings in the winter.

Cuttings can be taken as soon as the leaves drop and until about the end of March. If you've never experienced the magic of rooting a plant from a cutting, this is the best way to start. Hardwood cuttings are quick, easy and the most reliable of all the different types of cuttings. What's best is that you can forget about them entirely, except for summer watering, from the time you take them until the following winter.

There are a few simple rules, but it's amazingly easy to create new plants from old. It's incredible to think that a whole new plant can be produced from simply breaking a piece off one and sticking it into the ground, but it really does work, and we'd encourage anyone to attempt it.

Hardwood cuttings are taken from deciduous plants that are dormant in the winter. Equipment-wise, you need a sharp clean pair of secateurs, rooting hormone powder, containers and compost. The compost should be a free-draining mixture like a shop-bought seed and cuttings compost or a homemade mix of one part peat-free multipurpose compost to one part sharp sand or horticultural grit.

Above: Removing flowers is really important when taking a cutting. Here, a hydrangea flower is removed.

Now gather your plant material. Always choose the most healthy, vigorous shoot you can find – ideally you want the stem to be as thick as a pencil, depending on the parent plant. Whatever the plant, always take the strongest healthy shoots to propagate from; avoid material with flowers or buds attached as they will take the energy that the plant should be putting into producing roots.

It might not even be from your own garden. You might have admired a plant in a friend's or neighbour's garden – well, now's the time to ask for a cutting. We're always being asked what's the best time to take a cutting, and our favourite answer is

'When no one's looking', but it's best to at least attempt to ask.

The best cuttings come from stock that was hard pruned the previous year as these stems will be fresh and vigorous. Cut a section about 15 centimetres long for each cutting. Make a sloping cut at the top of the section of stem, just above a bud, and make a straight cut at the bottom of the section, just below a bud. Once you have separated the cutting from its parent, it is in danger of drying out, so get it potted up as soon as possible. If you can't pot it up straight away, put it in a plastic bag somewhere cold.

Dip the lower end – the straight cut – in some rooting hormone powder, which will encourage roots to shoot, and plant it in your container. You want about two-thirds of the shoot buried beneath the soil as roots will grow from these underground buds. The third above the soil will develop leaves in the spring.

If you are planting a few cuttings, set them 10–15 centimetres apart. Gently water them in using a hose or watering can with a rose attachment so that you do not dislodge the cuttings.

Now it's a game of patience. These cuttings will start to develop roots in the spring, but don't think about transplanting them until this time next year. Leave them in a cold frame or unheated greenhouse or somewhere with a bit of shelter and make sure they don't dry out.

Alternatively, it is possible to insert cuttings in the open ground, but check after a frost that they haven't been disturbed and firm gently back in if necessary.

What plants are suited to hardwood cuttings?

Shrubs that can be propagated through hardwood cuttings include:

+ Cornus (dogwood)
+ Salix (willow)
+ Ribes (flowering currants)
+ Spiraea
+ Kerria
+ Philadelphus
+ Viburnums
+ Roses

It's also an easy way of propagating fruits such as gooseberries and currants.

Perhaps the most exciting plant that can be successfully grown from hardwood cuttings are roses. Roses are nearly always sold as grafted or budded plants (grafting produces more reliable and consistent results for the grower), but they are happy to grow on their own roots.

Summer bulbs

While the best thing we can do for now is to continue dreaming of summer days, we can start planning for them.

Autumn is the main planting time for our spring flower favourites, but it's not until late winter or early spring that the summer bulbs appear in garden centres.

So what is a bulb? It's a plant that stores its energy underground as swollen base leaves, for example an onion. The term 'bulb' in gardening-speak also includes plants that are corms (such as gladiolus and crocosmia), which are swollen stem bases; rhizomes (such as cannas and the dreaded scutch or couch grass), which are swollen underground stems; and swollen root tubers such as dahlias or sweet potatoes.

Some bulbs that flower in summer are hardy and can be planted in the autumn, for example crocosmia, lilies and alliums – although these can also go in in the spring. But many are tender and need to be lifted out of the ground for the winter and stored somewhere dry.

Or they can be treated as annuals and planted fresh each spring. While you won't plant these out until the danger of frost has passed and the ground has warmed up, you can get things started in the greenhouse. So cannas, dahlias and begonias could all be started off indoors but won't go outdoors until late May.

Gladioli go straight in the ground as soon as it has heated up to about 13°C. Add some horticultural grit (a sharp stone mix) to the planting hole to keep their bottoms dry. Plant the largest bulbs 15 to 20 centimetres deep so that they won't need as much staking, and plant in succession, i.e. every week or fortnight, to keep up a constant supply of new flowers through the summer. Try 'Purple Flora', which has rich, dark purple, velvety flowers.

Dahlias have enjoyed a renaissance with the rise of the Instagram gardeners. They're not only great garden plants but also make wonderful cut flowers. Open-centred and single dahlias are best for wildlife. 'Night Butterfly' has intense deep red petals and a pink to white open centre, while 'Kelsey Annie Joy' produces orange-yellow flowers with a slight peach tinge to the centre of the flower. The Bishop series of dahlias – 'Bishop of Llandaff', 'Bishop of Canterbury' and 'Bishop of Auckland' – all have elegant flowers set against a dark foliage.

Cannas are a feature of hot borders and are a wonderful choice if you want to create a tropical effect or enjoy architectural planting – they have big banana-like leaves and very vibrant flowers in sizzling oranges, reds and yellows. Start them off early in the year inside and plant out when the last frost has gone. We'd recommend 'Wyoming', which has vibrant orange

flowers and luscious purple leaves, 'Black Knight' for its stunning scarlet flowers and 'Durban' for some very striking stripy orangey-green foliage.

And you could complete your jungle paradise with *Tigridia*, the tiger or peacock flower. Hardier varieties include *T. orthantha* 'Red Hot Tiger', or for a really vibrant burst of colour, try *T. pavonia* 'Lilacea'.

Above left: Dahlia 'Pacific View'.
Above right: Dahlia 'Honka Black.
Right: 'Night Butterfly'.

Snowdrops

PAUL

I'm a little biased as a galanthophile who's been in recovery for years, but I've fortunately recently relapsed. In the past I've worked in gardens with large collections of these fascinating spring bulbs and spent months propagating the small bulbs. My joy in these bulbs is their perfect timing.

The period immediately after Christmas can drag, especially if it's cold, damp and grey. In the first weeks of the year spring seems a long time off, but soon you'll see the first signs of life in the garden. And without fail, by the end of the month the snowdrops will be flowering and making gardeners smile.

The common snowdrop is a well-loved plant. Although not a native, it has made itself at home in these islands since at least the sixteenth century, happily naturalising in woodlands and gardens. It's frequently found in the estates of the oldest monasteries and church grounds and its clean white flowers are a symbol of hope and purity.

Galanthus nivalis, the common snowdrop, is the most widespread and best known. It's a solitary nodding flower with three white outer petals and three inner segments with some green markings. There are hundreds of cultivars and hybrids of this and other *Galanthus* species, with subtle variations in the size, shape and marking of petals, as well as differences in flowering times. Some collectors and enthusiasts enjoy and celebrate these differences so much that they are known as galanthophiles. While snowdrop enthusiasm isn't as mad as tulip mania in 17th-century Amsterdam, where tulip bulbs were traded for the price of homes, nonetheless a single snowdrop bulb, *G. woronowii* 'Elizabeth Harrison', was sold for £725 a couple of years ago, due to its rare yellow markings.

At the bleakest point in winter these small flowers shine. Yes, the differences are subtle and sometimes impossible for the untrained eye to identify, but there is a real joy in seeing them pop up and they're an utter delight on a sunny late winter morning, and they provide much-needed early pollen for the few brave pollinators that are out and about in January and February.

How best to grow snowdrops? As with any other plant, it's best to replicate their natural habitat. In this case, it's woodland planting, so semi-shade is ideal, and they like a humus-rich, slightly

Opposite, top: *Galanthus* 'Kildare'.
Opposite, middle: *Galanthus* 'John Long'.
Opposite, bottom: *Galanthus* 'Spindlestone Surprise'.
Over: A drift of snowdrops.

sold in autumn tend to dry out entirely and die. Nurseries will dispatch them in leaf, wrapped to preserve their moisture. Similarly, if you wish to lift and divide, do so while they are flowering or just after. If possible, plant where they have space to naturalise, as this shows them off at their best – tons of them scattered by nature's artistic hand – ideally at the base of a deciduous tree, where they will hide from May until next January.

If you'd like to dip a toe into the ocean of different varieties available, here's a few we'd recommend to start you off. *Galanthus* 'Magnet' is a taller, vigorous variety that quickly forms good clumps. 'Spindlestone Surprise' is one of the best and most vigorous yellows and when it forms a big clump will really stand out from its neighbours. 'Mrs McNamara' is one of the best early-flowering varieties, often coming into bloom on Christmas Day. Look out for 'S. Arnott' for honey-scented flowers – they're too low on the ground to get down and sniff, but a delicious fragrance to catch on a breeze.

To see a spectacular display of snowdrops, Altamont Gardens in County Carlow is well worth an early spring trip, as is Bellefield House in Offaly. In the UK, Dunham Massey Hall in Cheshire, Anglesey Abbey in Cambridgeshire and the Cambo Estate in Fife are all worth a look.

moisture-retentive soil. Plant them 'in the green'. This means when they are still in leaf. The bulbs are so small that the ones

February

In February, venture outside and allow your hopes to build. Woodlands, lawns and parks are carpeted with the early signs of spring – the weather and our light levels are still bloody miserable, but by the end of the month it feels as though spring is on the way. February seems never-ending – it's Groundhog Day. But a few good days of dry weather does allow you to get out and enjoy the garden. And to prepare for the real joy of spring, which is just around the corner.

Opposite: A sample of hellebores in Paul's garden.
Right: Frost on a February morning.

Fragrant February

DIARMUID

A whiff of sweet perfume drew me down the garden to the magnificence of a gorgeous Hamamelis mollis – the Chinese witch hazel. Despite being planted towards the end of my plot, the scent is so powerful you're forced to explore. The fragrance is emitted from the curious-looking flowers: four narrow yellow petals borne on the leafless branches in late winter.

While little else is happening in the doldrums of February there are some special shrubs to tempt and seduce us, ones that make our gardens more layered, complex and complete over an annual cycle. They are rare delights, plants that surprise and amaze. Plants that add so much to our garden story.

Witch hazels, which are native to the Far East, have in common delicate flowers with a beautiful fragrance, and their bark and leaves contain an astringent that is harvested for skin and beauty products. They are suitable for smaller gardens, as their eventual height and spread is only 1.5 to 2 metres. A witch hazel makes a lovely specimen in a pot on a patio, combined with some early spring bulb underplanting. It can then be moved 'back stage' in the garden during summer when it looks more ordinary. The Chinese witch hazel has sweetly fragrant, slender strap-like yellow petals and it's a parent to many cultivars with different-coloured flowers, for example *Hamamelis* × *intermedia* 'Jelena' has coppery orange petals and 'Diane' wonderful red flowers. Witch hazels prefer neutral to acidic soil but generally do well if the soil is humus-rich and well drained. They won't thrive on a shallow chalky soil and will do much better if sheltered from cold harsh winds.

Another shrub that provides winter scent is *Edgeworthia chrysantha*. A native of the Himalayas and China, it's commonly known as the oriental paperbush, as its bark is used for making high-quality paper. Japanese banknotes used to be made from this paper and were renowned for being difficult to forge. Fragrant tubular yellow flowers emerge from silky white buds, forming clusters of creamy yellow spheres on bare stems. It's not commonly grown, so it's perfect if you're looking for something a little out of the ordinary. Grow in moist, well-drained soil, ideally in a sheltered position as it doesn't like to go below -5°C. If your garden is prone to hard frosts, consider growing it in a pot in a cool conservatory or against a sunny south-facing wall. Even more striking perhaps is the cultivar 'Red Dragon' – equally fragrant but with orange-reddish flowers.

Opposite: *Daphne bholua 'Jacqueline Postill'.*

We're all familiar with the dazzling yellow forsythia that bursts into bloom in spring, but there's a much quieter white forsythia, *Abeliophyllum distichum*, which delights with its almond-scented delicate white or very pale pink flowers. Again, these deliciously fragrant flowers are borne on bare branches in midwinter. It may need some winter protection in colder areas, or you could plant one from the Roseum group, which has pink flowers and is hardier. Plant in full sun in a sheltered position near an entrance or pathway where you will get the full benefit of its winter scent. Native to Korea, it is an endangered species in the wild and close to extinction, so it's becoming rare and needs to be treasured.

With all these winter beauties, it's a good idea to locate them where you can see them from the house or, better still, near a path or front door so that you get to smell them every day.

Sarcococca (winter box) of all types should be considered. There's a lovely variety discovered by modern-day plant hunter Roy Lancaster in the 1980s. He chose a particular form he noticed flowering profusely by the Dragon's Gate Temple in Yunnan, naming it *S. ruscifolia* var. *chinensis* 'Dragon Gate'. It's a small plant, growing not much taller than a couple of feet, but it flowers without fail every year, and the flowers are followed by a profusion of red berries. Easier to source and no less beautiful is *Sarcococca confusa*. Being native to woodlands, it grows well in the deepest of shade, but can take nearly any position. It will grow away unassumingly for months, but when it flowers its sweet scent steals the show and always makes you do a double-take and hunt out the source.

A final plant that we think is the queen of winter scent is *Daphne bholua* 'Jacqueline Postill'. It's a small evergreen tree, best suited to a sheltered position, and prefers a slightly acidic soil. It flowers around the same time that snowdrops reach their peak and it's covered with beautiful pale pink flowers. The scent is the most intense of any winter plant and on a sunny, crisp winter's day it can really travel, filling the entire garden with a taste of what's around the corner in summer. Plant near a path where you can get up close and drink in the scent from these intensely fragrant flowers.

Opposite: *Sarcococca hookeriana* var. *digyna* 'Purple stem'.

Dividing herbaceous perennials

February is a great time to plant and plan and look back at what worked best in the garden last year. If there's a herbaceous perennial that did really well and you'd like to see more of it around the garden, the best way to achieve this is by dividing up the plant into smaller plantlets and replanting them. This is called lifting and division and is one of the easiest ways of propagating herbaceous plants.

Division is also necessary every few years to keep some herbaceous perennials fresh. Plants that form large clumps will eventually get tired and lose the vigour of their youth. The solution is to take the spade to them, and within a season that tired clump will be reborn. Once you divide out a plant and give it some new compost or feed it will explode, growing at an incredible rate and flowering with renewed vigour. Better again, you'll have more plants to spread into different areas of your garden and plenty to give away to gardening friends.

Heleniums and Michaelmas daises tend to grow out in concentric circles, leaving a woody old base at the centre. Think of a pebble dropped into a pond sending out ripples around it. The outer ripples are the fresh growth you want to harvest, while discarding the central woody base. Ideally you will lift and divide these plants every two to three years. Shasta daisies and phlox will benefit from annual division; other plants such as hostas, peonies and hemerocallis (daylilies), will happily clump along, performing well, without the need to disturb them.

The first rule of thumb is getting the timing right. Early-flowering perennials are best divided in autumn, late-flowering perennials in spring. Some good candidates for division now are heleniums, asters, eupatorium, rudbeckias and grasses. You can leave primula, brunneras, hardy geraniums and heucheras to flower now and

DIARMUID

Dividing flowering perennials on the long border in Glasnevin's National Botanic Gardens is a visceral memory for me. I was enchanted by the borders' seasonal development – almost bare during midwinter and just six months later a huge flourish of colour. In midwinter, when foliage and flower had died off and with little or nothing to be seen above the ground, we got to work. This involved digging up clumps of root, teasing away the roots of other perennials along with weeds such as bindweed or couch grass and diving and replanting the mother plant.

Opposite: *Rudbeckia fulgida* var. 'Goldsturm', a great candidate for dividing.

divide them in autumn. But the reality of any timing rule is that you will probably tackle the job when you have spare time or when the weather is clement enough to do so. Here, we like to use our mantra of 'the plant hasn't read the book', so divide plants when the opportunity presents itself, rather than waiting for the optimum time.

Dig up the plant you want to divide and shake off the loose earth so you can see what you are working with. Plants with a fibrous root system, like hardy geranium and astilbe, will break apart into plantlets quite easily. Others will require a bit more tugging and pulling – two garden forks back to back in the centre of the plant is a good way to tease apart thicker clumps like daylilies.

Below: Herbaceous borders at Altamont, County Carlow.
Opposite, top: *Illicium simonsii.*
Opposite, middle: *Illicium simonsii* flowers.
Opposite, bottom: *Illicium simonsii* fruit.

The sharp end of a spade is excellent for hacking through tough roots like hostas and agapanthus. Generally plants with thick fleshy taproots aren't so easy to divide and are better propagated via root cuttings, for example oriental poppies, lupins and acanthus.

You can plant your divisions in situ – creating drifts of your favourite perennials through the borders – but remember to keep them well watered while they establish themselves. It's a good idea to add some compost and fertilizer in the planting hole. You can also pot up the smaller plants individually and allow them to bulk up before planting them out next year.

Paul's plant of the month

Illicium simonsii
This is one of those lesser-known plants that I hope in the fullness of time will become a regular in gardens up and down the country. It has so many things going for it! It makes a small evergreen tree with a neat conical habit and its profuse primrose-yellow flowers are held on the leaf joints. Coupled with that is the fact that these flowers last a month and are followed by the most interesting fruit, very like star anise, which it is related to. It should not be used as a substitute for star anise, though, as it is poisonous! A real gem for a small garden.

How to design the garden of your dreams

February allows time for dreaming and planning ... for buying seeds and bulbs, for dreaming of new beds and borders or even whole new garden schemes. So what are the elements you need to consider when you start the design process?

Make an assessment – examine what you have

The first step is to make an assessment of what you have. Is it a couple of acres, a large plot that needs controlling, or is it a more intimate space, a suburban back yard?

Then, decide whether what you want is a hint of a new style or a complete makeover.

Next, observe the site and the conditions. This is crucial for understanding it and how good (or bad) a hand you have been dealt. What's the aspect, i.e. where is the sun at different times of the day?

Do you benefit from a lot of sun? Does your garden face north (a bit gloomy) or south (often sun-kissed)? Examine your soil. Is it light and loamy, free draining? Or is it heavy and plodding (which will be hard work)?

If you have a new garden, get to know it a little bit. Maybe even let it do its own thing over four seasons. See what emerges. Does that tree in the middle of the garden just block the view or will it be garlanded in pink petals in spring and become a feature you can't live without?

Then there are decisions to be made. Do you take away things, old features like rockeries, which can be fiddly to maintain, and is that unprotected garden pond going to be suitable if young children are visiting?

So many of these things will be hints that will advise you the road to travel along. To grow flowers and fruit and vegetables you want sun and good soil. But don't despair. If the site you are dealing with is on the shady side, for example, there are still plenty of pictures you can paint using plants that will thrive in such places.

Opposite: Diarmuid's garden transformation.
Over: Diarmuid's finished garden.

What's your garden style?

DIARMUID

For me it's definitely the jungle look. Inspired by the lush green planting in a local park, which was also a childhood playground, I find broad-leaved subtropical species appealing. Combining the leaf shapes and green tones into a picture is quite intoxicating.

Establishing a garden style is the first step in creating a garden design. Styles and design types have evolved over millennia in different parts of the world.

We're inundated with garden style influence. Since the arrival of cheap airfares, we have travelled lavishly and have seen cottage gardens, scenes of the Orient, Italian renaissance villa gardens and the splendour of Versailles.

The evolution of garden style has been a slow one. Aspects of different styles are regularly in displays such as the Chelsea Flower Show, so even without travel we can appreciate distilled versions of our favourites.

And in the digital era new trends take hold in double-quick time. So it's worth considering what garden style you love and what may work for you and your plot.

Oriental garden

Consider what you like. Is it an oriental garden, perhaps, with lots of green planting, bamboos, ferns, Japanese maples, variegated hostas, some gravel, possibly a pond or a stream with some fish and, peeping from behind a large shrub, the possibility of an eastern pavilion with a stone lantern to light your way?

Italian Renaissance style

Or perhaps on your travels you have seen Roman villas with their symmetrical parterres and mathematical planting? Space is divided by strict alignments of low evergreen hedges, fountains and statuary of Grecian goddess or Roman emperors cast in stone surveying their ordered landscape.

This neat, formal style can work very well even in small courtyard plots.

Cottage garden

Or do you pine for that chocolate-box vision of a cottage garden? Herbaceous flowers in a fruit salad of colour set behind the relaxed margin of a low box hedge, perhaps with fruit and vegetables planted in harmony, occupying the same space? Closing your eyes, you can picture the scene – lovely pink rambling roses creating an arch around the door and an apple tree dripping with fruit in late summer.

Cottage garden is an easy, pretty and relaxed style. It celebrates traditional plants and makes use of flowers that grow well in your area. It's colourful and great for small gardens.

The key elements of cottage garden style are lots of flowers, often mixed with grow-your-own veg and a fruit tree. Add in somewhere to sit, read or work. Garden furniture in a cottage garden doesn't need to match.

The New Perennial garden

Over the past twenty years the New Perennial movement has established itself as a contemporary trend, with waves of herbaceous plants married with grasses, swaying and dancing together as if in a field. This style favours large blocks of speckled colour, where plant combinations rather than other garden features are the focus.

Islamic garden style

Islamic gardens are lush oases of scent, water and sacred geometry. Often created within the protective walls of a courtyard, the style originated in ancient Persia.

The layout of a formal Islamic garden is known as a Charbagh. It comprises quadrants created by water channels or rills. They are surrounded by palm trees, olive trees, rose bushes, lemon trees and orange trees. Fragrant blossom plays a key role.

Wonderful original or restored examples can be found all over the world, including in India, Syria, Iran and Morocco. Some of the most famous are at the Alhambra in Spain.

Always planned as tranquil havens, their foremost role is to stimulate the senses in often private settings

PAUL

My favourite garden style is Irish country house gardening: colourful explosions of perennials and bulbs that combine to create quite a show.

Requirements – practicalities and desires

As someone planning a garden, you're in control of making space work. You are seeking to create a space that works horticulturally, where all the plants are in the right place and getting the light and growing conditions that they love, and where you are continually building a story as you wander around the plot until you arrive at your final focal point, when you stop and look back.

However small the plot, you can create interest along the way. The aim is to surprise and delight, to surround yourself in the beauty of nature and to entertain your garden visitor with something new at every turn.

Gardens are like dramas – there should be a few different layers and you should plan them properly, first setting the scene, then going on a journey, and finally reaching a resolution.

Make a plan

Making a plan is often very simple. Pace the plot – take rough measurements if you want and write them down on a sheet of paper. Chart your boundaries – where the house is, where your walls or fences are.

Now mark in any fixed features – an established tree, the space where your shed or greenhouse is and where the washing line is.

This is your template. It's an outline plan of your space. When you create the garden, you will be out there with a shovel and a fork and a wheelbarrow, digging away, creating new beds and altering paths.

Now use shape to create movement. Your objective, unless you are creating a small formal courtyard plot, is to take the eye away from the boundary and lead people on a journey. Sketching different shapes on paper will begin to show you possibilities.

The simplest is probably the C shape. Stand in the middle of the back of the house. Walking in a straight line is the fastest way to the end of the garden. But it's a little boring. Instead, do a banana walk – take a curved path around through your plot. Swing from one side of your garden down to the middle and back to the opposite side: a big C shape.

Top left: Renaissance garden style.
Top and above: Examples of Islamic garden style.

Then you can create a journey. When you're taking that walk and you can't see everything around you or ahead of you because your borders (i.e. the planting that you will be introducing) are full of volume, it will create interest and excitement.

If the plot is long enough you can join up two Cs going in opposite directions, creating an S shape with two dramatic curves. Once your borders are filled with voluminous plants, there will be no hint of what's around the corner.

Plan versus reality

Now take your sheet of paper outside and walk your plot. The trick will be to make the lines as simple but as dramatic as possible. If you are creating curves, put a big bend in them – go for a real walk through the site, not just from A to B.

Imagine starting at the corner of the back of your house and taking the longest possible walk to the corner on the same side at the end of your garden. Swing from your starting point to the centre of your garden – you should be hitting the opposite wall and then back again. Marking these lines out in the garden will involve using a hosepipe and a half-moon edger or a spade. Big sweeps are the key.

If you don't wish to use curved lines, plan a series of squares or rectangles, turned at an angle for the same effect.

The final step for your overall design is adding in the features. What will you see along the journey? This may be specimen plants such as beautiful trees that are set in borders and that become accents at appropriate times. Or you could use water – the sound of a trickle halfway down the garden will draw you on. And maybe a pavilion with its roof peeping up among the shrubs will act as your final focus.

Opposite: Alliums shine in this newly landscaped garden.

Soil

Soil is a wondrous thing, but it's often underappreciated. This remarkable resource sustains our lives. We owe our very existence to a 15-centimetre layer of soil and the fact that it rains. All our food comes directly or indirectly from the soil. Soil has been around for a very long time. Its formation begins with the combination of the breakdown of rock and the addition of organic matter. It takes hundreds of years to make a very thin layer and thousands to make the soil that we are all familiar with. It's the foundation of all gardening, good and bad, and respecting and improving it is the very basis of the craft of gardening.

Let's consider the different types of soil and begin to understand their different qualities. A little knowledge will help us to understand what we have and to improve our soil's health. This will enable the soil to sustain more life and allow us to grow better plants.

Grab a handful of soil and feel it in your palm. When you examine your handful of soil, you'll notice that it consists mainly of irregular particles. Science has classified these as sand, silt and clay particles. The difference between the three is size, nothing else. Clay is the most broken-down particle, silt is a halfway house and sand is the largest of the particles in the make-up of soil. Clay is pretty much microscopic, and sand particles are 0.05–2mm in size.

The other important constituent of soil is organic matter, which is anything that once lived – rotting trees, leaves, timber and anything else that once was alive and has died and returned to the soil. This is key. We can't change the soil formation process, but as gardeners we can add more organic matter, which will help improve whatever kind of soil we have. Soil is alive; hundreds of organisms, fungi and bacteria that are largely microscopic work away breaking down soil further and forming complex relationships. Trees in forests can communicate with each other through the fungus networks that surround all their roots.

The top layer of soil is known as the topsoil, below that is subsoil and below again is bedrock. How much of each of these you have depends on where you are and can vary greatly, even across a few miles, thanks to the effect of the last Ice Age. Most topsoil is about 25–45 centimetres deep and this is plenty to grow any plants a gardener will ever want to.

Acidic and alkaline soil

For us gardeners one important consideration is whether our soil is acidic or alkaline. Most plants will happily grow in a neutral to acidic soil. There are a few plants that specifically require acidic conditions, such as rhododendrons and certain heathers. Others will react and grow differently depending on the soil type they grow in. The common mophead hydrangea produces bright pink flowers when it is grown in alkaline soil, vivid blue flowers in acidic soil, and in soils closer to neutral it always attempts to take on both colours, resulting in a mottled effect. You can get simple test kits in garden centres that will tell you whether your garden is acidic, neutral or alkaline.

Soil types

Put simply, there are three main types of soil for us gardeners to be concerned about – sandy, loam and clay. In reality this is quite a complex subject, but for the purposes of growing plants there are a few basic rules that you need to know, so we'll try to simplify the whole thing.

Sandy

Sandy soils are quite often, but not exclusively, found in coastal areas. They are, as you'd expect, quite sandy. This means that they are extremely free draining, which can be a huge advantage, particularly in winter. If you have a garden with sandy soil you can work in it pretty much all year round. However, these soils don't hold on to nutrients particularly well and their biggest flaw is that they dry out very quickly in prolonged periods of drought.

Loam

Loam soils are every gardener's dream. They are basically soils made up of equal parts sand, silt and clay. They have the perfect balance of all three particles to make them the most versatile of all the soils you will come across. They are easy to dig and can be worked on most months of the year.

Clay

Clay soils aren't a total nightmare, but they are certainly harder work than other soils. They are made up of the smallest of the particles mentioned above and have great nutrient holding capacity, meaning that they are very fertile. Some plants, such as roses, thrive in them. They are hard to dig and work, though, and care should be taken to avoid walking on them too much in the winter as they are prone to waterlogging.

Improving the soil

The Touch Test

To test for the soil type you have you can do various experiments, but let's go back to our touch test. Take up a handful of soil and feel it. This tells you a lot about the soil. If it breaks up easily, doesn't stick together particularly well when compressed and is gritty to the touch, it's likely a sand-based soil. If it's easy to squash into a ball and sticks together well, but then breaks up easily, it's likely a loamy soil. If it remains in whatever shape you compress it to and smears and dirties your hands as you feel it, it probably contains lots of clay.

Whatever issue your soil has can be dealt with by the addition of organic matter. Compost, farmyard manure, composted bark – any organic matter will help. It will loosen a clay soil, helping it, in time, to drain better, and it adds substance to dry or sandy soils. It's a foolproof way to improve your soil and your garden. It's important to do this as you plant too, as this may be the only opportunity you'll have to get in and add significant quantities of material. While liquid feeds and fertilizers are like fast-acting energy drinks for plants, if you want endurance and long-term healthy plants, adding compost or farmyard manure is the best approach.

Only add well-rotted/broken-down material. Fresh sawdust, wood chippings and farmyard manure can actually be harmful to garden plants as they break down, so make sure that they've been composted for at least a year before you add them to your soil.

Avoiding walking on clay soils or wetter sites in the winter is important as compaction can cause a lot of damage to those micro-organisms we mentioned earlier. A simple tip to protect your soil is not to leave it bare. Nature doesn't do bare soil: over time it will always cover up a bare patch, and this helps prevent the soil being eroded and nutrients being leached from the soil.

Opposite: Soil preparation is key.

Bulbs

We love spring bulbs, and for good reason – a relatively small investment can bring such great joy to the garden at this time of year, when little else is growing. They begin to perform from this month on, peaking in March and April. They are magical and come in all shapes, sizes and colours imaginable. Some, such as the giant *Allium* 'Globemaster' and crown imperial, are huge and tower over everything; others, like scilla and dwarf daffodils, are compact and add delicate bursts of colour to the spring garden.

You plant them all the same way – in good, fertile, well-drained soil in the autumn. Dig a hole and drop them in. That's it! Generally speaking, two to three times the depth of the bulbs is a good planting depth. Even if you don't get them in at the right depth, they have an amazing ability to correct their own depth in the ground.

Below: *Allium hollandicum* 'Purple Sensation'.

We'll chat more about the technicalities of planting bulbs in our November section, but for now simply relish in the delight that bulbs bring to the spring garden. Observe, make notes and take pictures, ready for your autumn bulb order.

When using bulbs, what you're trying to achieve is a good succession of colour, starting with flowers as early as possible. With some careful planning, you can have spring-flowering bulbs that will bring colour to your life from January through to May.

Where to plant

It's also worth considering where you want to plant bulbs in the garden. Bulbs are adaptable and suited to a number of places. Areas under trees often lend themselves perfectly to bulb-planting. The ground under trees will be bare and open from leaf fall in autumn until leaf burst next May, so it's an ideal place to put in some low-growing spring bulbs.

When naturalising bulbs in grass it's important that you allow them to die off before you cut the grass. This can be as late as June if you have daffodils. For some gardeners this is harder than others, but do be patient. It will be worth the messiness next spring. Don't be tempted to tie up the foliage or chop it to keep it tidy either – just leave it. If you plant your daffodils among other plants, you won't even see it. Bulbs are great for filling gaps, especially in spring before other plants have their leaves fully out.

PAUL

In my Carlow garden, snowdrops and Crocus tommasianus *have been naturalised in the poor grass beneath a row of birch trees and they thrive there, lighting up the area on a February day. In time I'd like to add other spring delights such as glory-of-the-snow (*Chionodoxa luciliae*) and scillas. Daffodils are brilliant for naturalising too, but I avoid them here as I only want low-growing bulbs that flower early.*

Types of bulbs

PAUL

I also plant some alliums in the borders as I love the combination of purple balls above green swathes of plants in May. These May blooms will be preceded in March and April in my gardenr by a smattering of Narcissus triandrus 'Thalia', a fragrant white daffodil.

Tulips

Reliable tulips include 'Queen of the Night', with its rich plummy-purple colour; *Tulipa viridiflora* 'Spring Green', a very elegant cream with fresh green stripes; and 'Fly Away', which has the most fantastic scarlet goblet-shaped flower with golden yellow edges – a pure delight! 'Purple Prince' brings bursts of deep purple and tends to persist in a free-draining soil for a few years. Some tulips will return year on year, but many disappear, especially in damper areas, so to be sure of a display, you are best treating them as annuals and planting yearly.

Alliums

We like *Allium hollandicum* 'Purple Sensation', with its round balls of pinkish-purple flowers; *Allium cristophii* 'Star of Persia', globes covered with star-shaped violet flowers; and *Nectaroscordum siculum*, Sicilian honey garlic, which has umbels of gently nodding bell-shaped flowers.

Bulbs in pots

Bulbs are perfect for containers. They are compact, come in lots of dwarf forms and don't have massive root runs. They won't really need much watering until they begin to put on lots of growth and the sun comes out in spring.

Pots around the front door could be planted with a selection of dwarf bulbs such as *Iris reticulata* and *Muscari*, the grape hyacinth. There is a yellow grape hyacinth called 'Golden Fragrance' that is highly scented, so that would be perfect in a pot by your front door. Follow on with both dwarf and large daffodils and any tulip variety whose colour takes your fancy. You can be as brave as you dare with your colour combinations. It's your front door, after all!

Opposite: A pot full of daffodils brings much-needed spring cheer.

Spring pruning

Who doesn't love going on the attack in the garden, cutting, shearing, shredding – all for a great garden renewal? It can be a dark art, though, and people new to gardening are often unsure about what to prune and when.

Let's look at the basics. First, how you prune is important. Clean, sharp cuts are important, as torn or badly pruned stems can give easy access routes to pests and disease. After this you need to think about the three Ds – dead, diseased, damaged. Remove any dead, diseased or damaged branches, and then look out for any branches that are crossing or growing inwards. This will depend on what you are trying to grow, but, as a rule, branches that grow into the middle of the plant and cross or rub with others can be an issue and they are best removed, especially on smaller plants that you are training.

Reasons to prune

There are many different reasons to prune. In the natural landscape, wind or grazing animals can do the 'pruning'. Often plants will prune themselves, dropping off lower branches as they mature and holding on to the younger, more productive ones.

In our gardens, we generally prune to keep a tree or shrub restricted in size or to encourage flowers or fruits on new shoots. We also prune to get rid of dead or diseased wood and to help train leading shoots to cover walls or structures.

Equipment

Loppers are essential – long handles save a lot of bending and stretching and can attack those branches that are too big for secateurs. If you really want to take off large branches, go for a pruning saw – and be careful.

Keep tools sharp and oiled. Whatever tools you are using, try to ensure that the blades are kept sharp, so that the cuts are clean and sharp.

What to leave

From now until the end of March is your last chance to prune some species – before growth really takes off. But first – what not to touch? Basically, anything that is coming into flower or about to flower, such as forsythia, ribes, evergreen ceanothus, philadelphus and weigela – if you prune them now you will be left without any blossoms. Wait until they have finished flowering; then you can cut back and, on older established shrubs, completely remove about one-third of the old stems.

Ornamental cherries, plums and almonds should also not be touched – generally they don't need pruning anyway, but if it is necessary, leave it until late summer. There's a risk of silver leaf disease if you cut wounds in these plants now.

Birch should also be left until late summer or early autumn as it will bleed in spring as the sap rises. It's best to avoid pruning rhododendrons and camellias. Also leave daphnes, except to deadhead and take off any badly placed branches after flowering.

PAUL

Secateurs are one of the most frequently lost items in the garden. Diarmuid and I have differing opinions on this – he'd need a metal detector to recover them from all the places he's left them down, so he buys loads of cheap ones. I try to get really good ones, with a holster, and look after them. A can of aerosol oil usually frees them up when they've been accidentally composted.

What to trim

Summer-flowering shrubs

Summer-flowering shrubs, such as fuchsia, spiraea, perovskia, lavatera, buddleja and deciduous ceanothus (e.g. 'Gloire de Versailles') usually flower on new growth, so a good chop now will stimulate plenty of this new growth and flowers. If you do this too early in winter, the plant will produce tender new growth just at the time when it will be most susceptible to frosts. Simply put, you want to remove most of last year's growth – just leaving one or two buds – without cutting back into older wood. However, fuchsia can be cut back hard, nearly to ground level.

Shrub roses fall into this category too, so if you haven't pruned them yet, do so now to turbo boost them into growth and flowering later on. The same applies to late-summer-flowering clematis – these can be cut right down, almost to ground level, to just above a pair of buds.

Evergreen toughies

There's a group of evergreen toughies that are probably in most gardens. Landscapers love them because they are so hardy, but they can get very overgrown. If you have some of these that look way too big, you can cut them down to size now – *Aucuba japonica*, hypericum, euonymus, laurels, *Viburnum tinus*, box and hollies will all take a hard pruning, almost to ground level if needed. Yew can also be cut back hard, but don't try this with other conifers as they do not respond well to pruning!

Shrubs with colourful stems

Shrubs grown for colourful stems such as cornus (dogwood) and salix (willow) can be cut back hard to promote fresh stems, as can *Eucalyptus gunnii* if you grow it for its stems and juvenile foliage. And if you've any energy left, bamboos will just need dead stems removing – cut them out completely at ground level.

If you find yourself pruning the same plant year after year and complaining that it seems to be constantly outgrowing its space, maybe it's time for a rethink? Pruning is a human solution to controlling nature. It might be better to replant with something better suited to the space than to fight against a plant that wants to take over the space. Our 'right plant, right place' mantra is fitting here.

Opposite: An unruly flowering forsythia ready for pruning after flowering.

March

March is the month that pretends to be spring. For four weeks, only yellow is acceptable in the garden. For the rest of the season lots of gardeners turn their noses up at the idea of a yellow flower! The soil may be slowly warming up, but the weather can be unpredictable, with all four seasons in a single day. But it's time to start planting.

Opposite: A selection of Paul's daffodils.
Right: A delightful spring border.

Paul's plant of the month

Clematis cirrhosa 'Wisley Cream'

Clematis are fantastic climbers. It's such a large and diverse group that there's one for every season. There are lots to delight in summer, but a few are even winter-flowering. 'Wisley Cream' is one such example. It can flower as early as November but most likely will bloom from January through to March. It's evergreen and the leaves bronze up in winter too. The flowers aren't as large or impressive as its showy cousins, but it brings some much-needed cheer to the winter garden before disappearing into the background for the summer months.

Cut flowers

In the grand old days of enormously wealthy estate owners, walled gardens were created to provide not only fruit and vegetables for the house but also flowers for cutting and display in reception halls, grand dining rooms and on dressing tables. And out of this emerged the tradition of head gardeners competing to show the best chrysanthemums, sweet peas and roses, among others. Flowers cut from the garden were a thing.

In recent years the emergence of the supermarket has turned cut flowers into another commodity, produced as cheaply as possible. Whole industries have been created in which flowers are farmed in far-flung places, often using scarce local resources, and flown to our shops and supermarkets. It's an ecological nightmare.

For all these reasons it makes sense for us to grow some of our own flowers for cutting, especially when we are so lucky with the relatively mild climate that we enjoy on these islands. More and more people are beginning to realise this and in recent years small growers of seasonal flowers have emerged to supply local markets, so even if you don't grow your own flowers for cutting, keep an eye out and support a local grower.

Lots of us will wander into the garden with the secateurs and snip off a few blooms for the occasional display, but it is possible to turn an area of the garden, maybe even the veg patch, to growing flowers designed only to be cut. They can be grown, as was traditional, in lines or, in a much less structured way, in patches of the garden.

Opposite: A selection of cut flowers from Diarmuid's garden.

The best flowers for cutting

Which plants are good for cutting and flower-arranging? The answer is a lot of them, but some do last longer and give far better value. That said, there is nothing wrong with going around your own garden at any time of the year and gathering a simple posy from whatever flowers and foliage look good; you will soon learn what lasts and what doesn't.

Bulbs

Daffodils, especially the dwarf varieties, make fantastic cut flowers. They naturalise easily in the garden so you can have plenty of flowers every year. Tulips also make great cut flowers, but you will probably need fresh bulbs every year to ensure good-quality flowers.

Annuals

+ The cheapest and easiest option is to raise annuals from seed; and there are so many plants to choose from.

+ Cosmos produces tons of flowers in gorgeous shades of pinks and white, and nigella (love-in-a-mist) will also reward you with many blooms.

+ Larkspur (*Consolida* spp.) is related to the delphinium. It's a hardy annual, so it can be planted straight in the ground where you want it to grow – and it's a delight in the cottage garden.

+ Sunflowers add drama and sunshine to any bouquet.

Opposite: A selection of cut flowers from Diarmuid's garden.

+ Scented flowers will give enormous pleasure indoors, so sow some *Nicotiana* – tobacco flowers.

+ The sweet pea is the queen of scent. It's the ideal cut flower, as the more you cut, the more flowers it will produce. You quite literally can't go wrong.

+ Annual grasses are great for some texture when it comes to arranging flowers and *Panicum miliaceum* 'Violaceum' not only looks great for months but provides seeds for the birds when it's gone over.

Perennial borders

Perennial borders can provide many elegant blooms.

+ Asters, astrantias, chrysanthemums and delphiniums are all good cut flowers.

+ Dahlias are really the king of cut flowers – they come in so many different varieties, shapes and colours – and better still, they flower right up until we have a good frost.

+ Roses are a must; there is nothing more beautiful in a bouquet than garden roses in varying stages of bloom.

+ Hydrangeas, with all their old-fashioned glamour, are making a comeback.

Evergreen foliage

+ Evergreen foliage is useful, and eucalyptus is a must-have. *E. gunnii* can be cut back regularly to provide fresh foliage.

How to cut and arrange flowers

The best time to pick flowers is in the morning, when their stems are full of water. If you can't get out first thing in the morning, wait until evening. What you don't want to do is pick them in the full heat of day when they are water-stressed.

Immediately plunge the stems into a bucket of water. For longer-lasting vase life, re-cut the stems at a sharp angle and steep them in water for a couple of hours or overnight. Strip off any foliage below water level.

Now have fun arranging them – experiment with colour combinations, contrasting shapes, and raid your garden for foliage.

Right: Daffodils make fantastic spring cut flowers. **Opposite:** Delphinium is a perfect cut flower.

Planting vegetables

March isn't always the best month to get out in the veg garden, especially if the soil's wet, but it's the perfect time to plan and order your seeds to be ahead when the madness of the growing season kicks in. By month's end, spring really will have set in and your vegetable gardening year can begin in earnest.

With so much choice available, whether in shops, catalogues or online, it can be hard to decide which is best for you, especially if you're a gardening newbie.

Below: Kale in a raised bed.

For some, outdoor gardening space is limited to maybe a courtyard or balcony area that needs to be both productive and aesthetically pleasing. In these areas, fruit and vegetable plants should share growing space with ornamental species.

What to grow in a small space

Keep it simple and avoid crops that need trenches, such as celery and asparagus, or earthing up, such as leeks. Sprawling pumpkins and squashes and larger crops, such as Brussels sprouts, aren't generally suitable for smaller areas.

Cut and come again

Any of the 'cut and come again' crops are invaluable – you just pick a few leaves as you need them, and the plant will keep growing. They include lettuce, mustard, kale, chard and spinach, and are often sold together in seed packets as mixed salad leaves.

As you are not letting the plant mature, you can grow them tightly together. If you prefer a whole head of lettuce, try smaller varieties of butterhead and cos such as 'Tom Thumb' and 'Little Gem'. Dwarf green curly kale is a compact crop that you sow from April onwards, which provides healthy greens in the depths of winter. In fact, any dwarf variety of veg is useful when space is at a premium.

Courgettes

One plant that will work in a sunny space is a courgette plant. A single courgette plant in a large container will supply you with courgettes all summer long!

Potatoes

Potatoes can be grown in containers or grow bags, even on a balcony. Buy them as small tubers – one or two tubers will give a great yield. For small spaces we would recommend only growing early potatoes – these are quicker to mature and you avoid the problem of blight that can occur with maincrop varieties. In addition, when your harvest is finished in June and July, you get your space back, which you can use for late-summer salad crops. Good early potato varieties are 'Orla', Colleen' and 'British Queen'.

Broad beans

Broad beans are hardy and can be planted in autumn or spring, but French and runner beans are half-hardy, so they can only be planted outdoors in May, after the last frost. For smaller spaces, choose dwarf cultivars such as 'Hestia' and 'Pickwick' runners and 'Purple Queen' French beans – these can manage without any support at all.

Maximise your space

Vertical space

Use vertical space where available – perhaps a trellis on a wall or small bamboo wigwams – and grow climbers such as runner, broad and French beans, and peas. These crops are one of the best to grow your own as they taste so much better eaten straight after picking.

Baskets, buckets, dustbins ...

Hanging baskets, buckets and even old dustbins are a great way of maximising your growing space, particularly on a balcony. You could be harvesting pounds of cherry tomatoes later this summer. 'Hundreds and Thousands', 'Tumbler' and 'Tumbling Tom Red' are all bush varieties that don't require support or need their side shoots removed, so they will happily cascade from a hanging basket or a container.

Intercropping

Utilise any leftover spaces by tucking in some smaller crops – this is known as intercropping. You could sow a few radishes – one of the quickest seed-to-harvest vegetables there is – a couple of beetroot ('Boltardy' is your reliable choice here) and a handful of spring onions ('White Lisbon').

Windowsills

If you've no available outdoor space, you can use a windowsill. It's the ideal spot to grow herbs and have them within easy reach for when you're cooking. Basil, chive and parsley seeds can all be started indoors now until early April and when the soil warms up you can sow seeds of chervil and coriander directly into soil outdoors from March onwards. Pots of herbs can also look great arranged on small ladders against a wall.

Seedlings

Where space is extremely limited you might feel you don't have room for seed propagation – in this case you can buy many of the plants mentioned here as seedlings in garden centres during spring and take it from there!

Opposite, top: Raised beds are a great way to grow vegetables.
Opposite, above right: Potatoes are one of the easiest and rewarding vegetables to grow.
Opposite, right: Onions drying before being stored.
Opposite, left: Onions growing.

Spring-flowering shrubs

The saying goes 'when gorse is out of blossom, kissing is out of fashion'. Gorse really does flower all year round, but it peaks in spring. March's warming weather and sunshine lead to some shrubs shaking off the winter slumber and producing spring blossom. Joining the gorse are some very common garden plants – forsythia, ribes and kerria. They're anonymous for much of the year, but now is their time to shine.

Spring-flowering shrubs and trees are delightful plants to have in our gardens, cheering us up and anticipating a vigorous growing period. They provide structure, colour, foliage, scent and flowers and some of the most special ones can become a focal point for this time of year.

Chaenomeles japonica (Japanese quince)

While these plants peak from March to May, they can look great even in bud for all of January and February. A real old-fashioned plant and stalwart of cottage gardens, they really perform in early spring. They are tough, are easy to grow and come in pink, white, peach, red and yellow. The fruit can be cooked into a jelly. They do well in virtually any soil, and they also look great trained against a wall or a fence but require regular pruning to keep them there. There are some great examples of this in the National Botanic Gardens in Glasnevin.

Rhododendron barbatum

This is a most elegant rhododendron, with crimson flowers held aloft above handsome foliage. The stems have barbs or bristles, hence the name. An introduction by plant hunter Joseph Hooker from his trip to the Himalayas in 1850, it has the added advantage of ornamental bark – smooth and peeling in reddish and purple tones. In time it forms a small tree. As a plant that likes an acidic soil, it's not for every garden. It would love a woodland site where taller trees will shelter it from prevailing winds.

Corylopsis glabrescens (fragrant winter hazel)

Corylopsis is covered in the most fantastic primrose-yellow scented flowers for most of March. They

Opposite: A pot of rhododendron in Diarmuid's garden really stands out when it's in bloom.

are bell-shaped and hang in profusion from the branches. It's a large shrub that does best in an acidic soil and in some shelter. Prune after flowering if needed, but at the back of a large border or even in a woodland border they can be largely left to their own devices. The leaves also give good autumn colour.

Osmanthus delavayi

During March and into April, this is smothered in small white tubular flowers that create a cloud of fragrance to walk through. An evergreen shrub with small dark-green serrated leaves arranged in opposite pairs, it is great as a hedging plant or planted near a pathway or entrance. Its arching habit also makes it a good stand-alone shrub. Happy in the sun or shade, it does well in most soils. Clip if required after flowering.

Prunus 'Tai Haku'

This has the largest flowers of all the cherries – big single white blooms set against the just-emerging young bronzy foliage. If you have the space, plant in the sunshine in well-drained soil. Like other cherries, it's shallow-rooting, so it will lift the lawn if planted in the centre, and for the same reason it's definitely not suitable near paving.

Prunus incisa 'Kojo-no-mai'

If you haven't the space for a full-blown cherry tree but love them, this is the plant for you. It's a slow-growing shrub with slightly twisted branches that resemble a bonsai. In March it is covered in shell pink flowers with a slightly darker centre. It also has the most intense autumn foliage. A really stunning plant for a small space.

Exochorda × macrantha 'The Bride'

An aptly named shrub, as it looks like the full skirt of a bridal dress when it's smothered in large white flowers on arching stems that reach the ground. As a focal point it will dazzle for around six weeks from April.

Ribes sanguineum 'King Edward VII'

If pink is your colour, then a flowering currant is a must! It gives a magnificent display of dangling pink flowers, just as the plant comes into leaf. It can be pruned immediately after flowering and is extremely vigorous. It's often found in hedgerows where old cottages once stood. The leaves that follow have a strong currant smell. It's easily propagated from hardwood cuttings.

Halesia carolina (snowdrop tree)

Stand underneath the snowdrop tree when it's in full bloom and gaze up at the bell-shaped, nodding pure white flowers. It's just gorgeous. Preferring neutral to acid soil, this is an excellent choice for a small garden – dainty and unusual.

Spiraea 'Arguta'

Justifiably popular, this deciduous shrub bursts into clusters of flowers along arching stems, earning its common name of Bridal Wreath. It's easy to grow on most soils. Remember to clip back stems after flowering to ensure a great display every year.

Above: Lilac is a great spring shrub.

Climbers

One of the first steps when creating a garden is to disguise boundaries. It's especially important if you are surrounded by fence panels or concrete walls. And it's a project that can be undertaken at the earliest stages, even when you haven't made big plans for an overall design, or if the garden will be given over to the children for a few years as a football pitch or trampoline carrier.

Climbing plants are the first thing in vertical gardening – they help to melt the architecture of your home into your plot. They soften unsightly features and create a super environment for wildlife. However, they can take a bit of time and patience to get established.

Climbers are plants that have adapted their growth to climb towards the light, often using other plants to support them on their way upwards. So they are used to having their feet in the shade and their flowers are produced in the sunshine. Growing them among other plants will help keep their root run cool.

Planning and patience really are the key. Start off by considering what you want the plant to do. Would you go for something like an ivy that is dependable, that will take all sorts of abuse, that will grow even in a dry area and won't be bothered by shade? Or do you want something like a beautiful rose to adorn the outside of your country cottage?

There's a vast amount of choice – evergreen, deciduous, flowering and fruiting. But the trick is to understand the type of conditions that climbers love. Often climbers are planted at the base of a wall where the concrete and foundations suck in any available water. Be aware of this and remember that a new plant going into the ground is going to be a bit stressed. It's coming to you from perfect nursery conditions where its every need is tended to, and your environment might be comparatively inhospitable. So rather

DIARMUID

At home I've planted climbers to stand out as specimens rather than to clothe backdrops. I built a veranda onto the back of the house and planted wisteria, star jasmine, roses and evergreen clematis at the base of its supporting cast-iron pillars. And now, five years later, they are beginning to fulfil their potential, winding upwards, creeping along the railings and framing the upstairs windows with glorious foliage and flowers.

than planting right up against the wall, lead your new plant in on a bamboo cane from about 20 centimetres away from the wall. Taking time to prepare the soil is important, no matter what you are planting, so dig in plenty of good organic manure if possible. And water liberally in the first months.

Here are some delightful climbers that will inject colour and vertical excitement into your plot.

Annual

Eccremocarpus scaber (Chilean glory flower)

Sow seed indoors now and transplant outdoors after the last frost. It will soon gallop away and produce red and orange tubular flowers in early summer. It might overwinter in milder areas as it is a tender perennial, but in most areas you treat it as a half-hardy annual and sow seeds again in spring next year. It likes a moist, well-drained soil in full sun and will scramble up a fence, turning it into an exotic picture.

Cardiospermum halicacabum (balloon vine)

Hailing from the tropics, the wonder of this plant is in its seed pods, which hang down like green lanterns. Each contains black seeds with a perfect white heart imprinted on each, giving rise to another common name, 'Love in a Puff'. Grow as a half-hardy annual, sowing indoors now and transplanting outdoors in late May.

Rhodochiton atrosanguineus (purple bell vine)

The purple bell vine has magenta bells with a tubular dark-burgundy flower hanging from the centre. Sow seeds under glass now and transplant when there's no danger of frost. The flowers appear in late summer, a welcome sight when many of the garden's blooms have gone over. The foliage is made up of delicate heart-shaped leaves in a light green, which beautifully set the scene for the flowers.

Ipomaea (morning glory)

Morning glory 'Heavenly Blue' has absolutely wonderful heart-shaped leaves and the flowers are glorious blue funnels you want to dive into. Morning glory is also available in pink, maroon and white. It's closely related to the dreaded bindweed but with none of the disadvantages. Young plants can be planted outdoors after the last frost.

Opposite, above left: *Solanum crispum* 'Glasnevin'.
Opposite, above right: Wisteria in Diarmuid's garden.
Opposite, right: Honeysuckle in bloom.
Opposite, left: *Actinidia kolomikta,* with its white tips.

Deciduous

Lonicera periclymenum (honeysuckle)

The scent of honeysuckle, or woodbine, is one of the sweetest summer fragrances. If you have a spot where you like to sit and relax in the evening, plant honeysuckle nearby as its fragrance will be strongest at night-time; the plant uses it to attract pollinating moths. It is vigorous, so make sure it has space to ramble. This hardy deciduous climber is native to these islands and is commonly seen growing in hedgerows. Now's a good time to get planting hardy climbers such as this and clematis.

Hydrangea anomala subsp. *petiolaris*

The deciduous climbing hydrangea is now commonplace in garden centres, and rightly so. It flowers freely, will grow on a dark north-facing wall where nothing else will and clings on by itself, while never being too vigorous and getting out of hand. A win all round.

Actinidia kolomikta

Most people are amazed when you tell them that kiwis can be grown outdoors in this country. They are a woody vine and perfectly easy to grow. If you want fruit, you'll need a male and a female. 'September Sun' is a female clone and 'Arctic Beauty' a male one. However, this climber doesn't need to bear fruit to be of interest as when it matures the leaves take on the most fascinating characteristic: their ends turn white tinged with pink as if someone has dipped half of each leaf into poorly mixed pink paint. It really can light up a dull wall in the garden.

Evergreen

Hardenbergia violacea (vine lilac)

This is also known as the happy wanderer, and it carries violet-blue pea-like flowers from early in the year. It hails from Australia and in its homeland will grow as an evergreen climber. In these parts it will only survive winter outdoors in milder areas, but you can grow it under glass from seed in spring and enjoy its flowers in early summer, or it can make a lovely conservatory plant.

Solanum crispum 'Glasnevin' (Chilean potato vine)

As its name suggests, it's closely related to the potato. It creates a wonderful display in the garden, its violet-coloured flowers with yellow centres flowering for most of the summer. It's vigorous and needs support but makes a really dramatic climber in the right position.

Pileostegia viburnoides (climbing hydrangea)

One of many plants that come under the climbing hydrangea category. This self-clinging climber has masses of fluffy white flowers that dust the plant from top to bottom in late summer. It's evergreen and a slow plant to establish but very well behaved. It can be pretty much left to its own devices, save for chopping it annually when it has reached as far as you want it to.

Opposite: Climbing hydrangea clings to a building.

Spring containers

Planted pots and containers brighten up entrances to homes and provide instant colourful displays in prominent garden spots such as patios or around garden features.

Rather than making off-the-cuff choices in the garden centre, plan for a wonderful combination of planting. If you decide on a theme and possibly even a succession of colours, you will be rewarded by a beautifully coordinated display from spring into early summer.

We take inspiration from Danish gardener Claus Dalby who produces the most magnificent displays of tiered pots outside his property. Claus plans and plants beautiful colour schemes, often using just one or two colours in different hues, for example rows of pale cream tulips, white tulips and white daffodils, all to great effect.

Containers are an excellent way to capture the fleeting nature of some spring plants, especially tulips. Pots crammed with tulips can take centre stage outside your front door for the month they are at their best and then be discreetly removed while you allow their foliage to die back. They can then be planted out in the garden or stored out of sight until next year. And waiting in the wings is your next batch of pots of colour.

Here are some ideas for spring containers.

Opposite, left A winter/spring pot display.
Opposite, right: Lasagne pots bursting with crocus.

White and yellow schemes

A fresh and elegant combination and a classic Easter display. Create using white and yellow daffodils, both miniature and regular sizes, along with yellow and white tulips – these are all available in pots now in garden centres. Add hellebores, which will keep flowering well into May, or, for smaller pots, you can use pristine white *Bellis perennis* and lots of primroses and polyanthus – pack them in for maximum impact!

Yellow and blue

Yellow and blue create a colourful contrast. The blues could be violas, brunnera, *Omphalodes*, gentian, muscari and anemone. Pair with yellow wallflowers, *Narcissus* 'Tête-à-Tête' and primulas. And for an ornamental planter that offers something extra, pop in some herbs such as sage and rosemary; they are great in kitchen window boxes, within easy reach for cooking.

Pinks and purples

Pink and purple flowers bring warmth and cheer and complement each other beautifully. In smaller spaces, use pretty little alpines such as *Arabis alpina* and *Dianthus*. Contrast different pot sizes of pink and purple tulips. Bleeding heart (*Lamprocapnos spectabilis*, formerly *Dicentra spectabilis*) is one of our top spring plants and deserves a pot all of its own, all the better to admire its arching stems dripping with heart-shaped pink flowers.

Foliage

A green foliage scheme can be very pleasing. Experiment with different shades of green, such as lime-green *Heuchera* 'Marmalade', yellowish-green *Acorus gramineus* 'Ogon' grass and *Carex oshimensis* 'Evergold'. Baby tree ferns (*Dicksonia antarctica*) look beautiful in pots and are a more affordable way of acquiring this statuesque fern. You could also use baby *Astelia chathamica* 'Silver Spear' with its wonderful silvery leaves as part of a temporary display and then plant it out in the garden for permanent pleasure.

Above: Colourful spring pot displays.

April

April means business. The explosion of growth in our gardens this month is incredible. After sulking for months on end there's a complete transformation almost overnight. Daffodils finish, tulips blossom and all those myriads of spring plants really shine. Your spring garden will be at its best, packed with primroses, hellebores, wood anemones and any number of bulbs. Avoid having to play catch-up later by spending some invigorating weekends working your plot.

Opposite: Floating auriculas and primrose.
Right: Auricula flowers catch everyone's attention.

Mixed borders

PAUL

In my garden, any colour goes. If Gertrude Jekyll's ghost ever visited, she would be perplexed. I let all colours clash and enjoy the random mix of colours that happens when you focus solely on the plants and not on the colour of the flower. Nature isn't concerned about colour combinations, and neither am I. Even Diarmuid agrees!

Opposite: Paul's Garden.

Things to consider

Location
Location is primary. If you have a nice open and sunny position, that will be ideal. You may, however, be gardening in the shade, which will determine your plant choices.

Soil
Prepare the soil by digging it over to remove any weeds, and improve its structure and fertility by adding compost or well-rotted manure.

Colour theme
Will you have a colour theme? The renowned English gardener and artist Gertrude Jekyll liked to run colours from cool whites and blues right through to warmer reds and oranges; and Vita Sackville-West created an all-white garden room at Sissinghurst. Observe other people's planting schemes, imagine different colour combinations – contrasting, complementing and clashing. For many this is what gardening is all about.

Shapes
You also want to create different shapes – this will be achieved through a mixture of shrubs, evergreen and deciduous, perhaps small trees, such as a Japanese maple, as well as your perennial plants. Shape will be the backbone of your border, providing structure and substance year long. Plants you can use to achieve this include box, skimmia, hydrangeas, phormium, azaleas, rosemary and bay trees. The bays and box could also be clipped into cones, balls or other shapes depending on the style of the garden.

Textures
Consider the different textures – soft feathery plumes of grasses, strong shapes like hosta leaves, the jagged serrations of *Melianthus*,

architectural acanthus leaves and frothy fern fronds. And try to incorporate different flower shapes: globes of alliums; daisy-like coreopsis, anthemis and rudbeckia; spikes of veronica; and bell-shaped foxglove and campanula. Different heights will create a rhythm in your border. Tall spires of *Ligularia*, lobelia, red hot poker, foxtail lilies and white willow herb contrast beautifully with softer mounds of hardy geraniums, *Alchemilla mollis* and lavender. Think about when these plants will come into flower so that the pairings you imagine synchronise in reality. And don't forget about late summer – sedums, leucanthemums, penstemon and crocosmia will all extend your colour season.

The golden rule

When you've made your final selection, the golden rule is to plant in uneven numbers. Groups of three or five of the same plant always create the most pleasing effect to the eye. Repeat-planting of the same species at another position in the border, even several times, will create a unity. Find out how big the plant will become and give it sufficient room to reach its final size. Gaps can be temporarily filled with your favourite bedding plants and annuals.

Your mixed border will now be packed with enough flower power to create explosions of colour as well as beautiful shrubs to create year-round interest.

Don't be afraid to try new things. Gardens are ever-changing and you'll constantly be digging and swapping plants once you get bitten by the garden bug.

Opposite: A mixed border with trees, shrubs, topiary and perennials.

Tulips

April is tulip season, a wonderful time of the year. With tulips, you are spoilt for choice – they range from the most striking reds and purples to dreamy pastels, and you can use all sorts of combinations too.

However, there are a few other factors to bear in mind. Tulips can begin flowering in early spring and some, such as the late singles – for example the wonderfully dark 'Queen of the Night'– will flower up to early summer. By mixing the types you can extend the tulip season so that for the entire month of April you'll have a tulip in flower.

DIARMUID

Tulips stand to attention – and demand our attention through the month of April. They're both familiar and exotic and arrive in a range of colours, forms, sizes and effects. My favourite are the parrot cultivars with their curvy, wavy petals – the blue and black ones especially.

Flower shapes

There is also some versatility when it comes to flower shapes. Diarmuid's favourites are the parrot tulips, but you may prefer the classic vase shape of the Triumph tulips – for example, the glorious 'Princess Irene' in her cloak of orange and purple. Double-flowered tulips can be exceptionally pretty and are often compared to peonies because their petals are so blowsy and extravagant. 'Angelique' is one of the best known; it's a delightful concoction of pale pink and cream, beautiful for cutting and indoor display

Durability

Durability is also a consideration. Many highly bred tulips will only last a season. In areas that have free-draining soil that doesn't get waterlogged in winter they may rebloom the following year but not always as big or as brightly. For this reason, gardeners often treat tulips as annuals and replant fresh batches each year. However, species varieties such as *Tulipa clusiana* and *T. turkestanica* will naturalise and spread. Good old-fashioned Darwin hybrids, which are generally red, pink or yellow, are also quite reliable and are sometimes called perennial tulips as they will perform for a few years.

If you do leave tulips in the ground, I'd recommend feeding them next spring. Those planted in sunny, well-drained areas that get a good summer baking have the best chance of flowering for a couple of years. You can also improve chances of reflowering if you lift the tulips after flowering when all the foliage has died back and store them somewhere warm before replanting next autumn.

Below: Species of tulips naturalised in grass.
Bottom left: Bold, contrasting tulip colours.
Below left: A jolly display of mixed tulips in a spring border.

Hardy annuals

There's a beautiful range of hardy annual seeds that will produce blossoms to delight you in the summer. Annuals are plants that complete their life cycle in one season, i.e. they germinate, grow, flower and set seed all in one growing season.

Hardy annuals are simply annual plants that aren't frost-tender so there is no risk of them being damaged by later frosts. They're relatively easy to grow, and as the ground warms up you can plant them directly into the soil or into pots, so you won't need a greenhouse or space indoors to germinate them. They are inexpensive (or free if you collect seed as it ripens in autumn) and hugely satisfying to watch develop over their short life cycle.

To successfully grow them you will need a weed-free, finely raked, crumbly soil. All will flower better in an open, sunny position. Sow as per packet instructions and water in gently.

Opposite: A mix of hardy annuals form this annual pollinator meadow.

Ratibida columnifera f. *pulcherrima* 'Red Midget' (prairie coneflower)

'Red Midget' is a cheerful flower that is also known as Mexican hat and as prairie coneflower. It has yellow and maroon petals and a distinctive cone-shaped centre. It flowers from June to September, does well in a dry soil and makes a good cut flower.

Papaver somniferum (opium poppies)

You could just grow a bed of poppies and be happy! Wonderful cultivars include 'Black Beauty', which has dark – almost black – peony-like blooms, and 'Victoria Cross', which has fringed red petals and a white cross in the centre. Their seed pods look beautiful too – a particularly distinctive variety is 'Hens and Chicks', in which the central pod is surrounded by baby pods.

Nigella damascena (love-in-a-mist)

This is an old cottage garden favourite that never fails to delight with its combination of ferny foliage and pretty blue flowers. 'Miss Jekyll' is one of the best-known strains. It will happily self-seed, so get the cycle going this year.

Moluccella laevis (bells of Ireland)

A firm favourite with flower arrangers for its bell-shaped green flowers, which can be successfully cut and dried. The fresh green is a good companion for more brightly coloured annuals and will look very cool alongside white flowers.

Clarkia/godetia

Clarkia or godetia is an easy-to-grow annual with silky petals in pinks, lavenders and pale purples. This Californian native will bring colour and joy to your garden and make pretty floral posies for your vases.

Nicandra physalodes (shoo-fly plant)

The shoo-fly plant has bell-shaped lavender flowers followed by black seed pods that look a bit like Chinese lanterns. One seed will grow into a bushy plant, so it's a handy space filler.

Centaurea cyanus (cornflower)

Cornflowers evoke meadows and hazy summer days. However, this beautiful native is in decline in the countryside, so to be sure of seeing it this summer, sow it in your own garden. Wonderful piercing-blue flowers make excellent flowers for cutting as well.

Nasturtiums

Nasturtiums are ideal for absolute beginners – the big seeds are easy to handle and germinate quickly. Their distinctive foliage is easy to recognise as it emerges, and the reward is tons of flowers in orange, yellow and red. The flowers also make zesty and colourful additions to salads.

Lawn alternatives

The biggest drawback to lawns is the lack of pollinating flowers for bees, butterflies and other beneficial insects. As we cut lawns so regularly, the grasses don't get a chance to flower and the 'weeds' that appear, such as dandelions and daisies, also get their heads chopped off as soon as they dare to pop up. Or worse, we kill them with weed killer. Add to that the energy costs of lawnmowers, the need for sprinklers to keep the lawns green in high summer and fertilizers applied to get that emerald sheen, it's probably time to examine the alternatives.

The simplest solution is to stop mowing and let a natural meadow form. At the very least you will get flowering grasses. If there are any weeds that you don't like, you can remove them by hand and you can add in wildflower plugs or seeds to introduce some colour. On richer soils, grasses generally outperform wild flowers, so a really floriferous meadow can be hard to obtain. One method is to introduce a semi-parasitic plant such as yellow rattle (*Rhinanthus minor*). This is a yellow-flowered annual plant that hoovers up nutrients and water and thereby reduces the vigour of grasses, allowing other annuals to have a chance to flower. There's more on wildflower meadows in the July section.

On larger areas, you could mow a pathway through the meadow, which is both practical and gives a pleasing contrast between clipped and unmown grass. Later in the summer, once the flower and grasses have set seed, you can cut the meadow. You'll still need to cut a meadow, but once or twice a year will be sufficient.

DIARMUID

In spring 2020 I decided to dig up my lawn and replace it with plants and a mini ecosystem that would be more sustainable and healthier for our planet. Lawns are relatively cheap to lay but expensive to maintain. They have a place in our gardens, but maybe they shouldn't be everywhere. And we should possibly re-examine the exacting standards we expect from them.

Thyme

If your soil is free-draining and in a sunny position, how about a thyme lawn? Popular in Edwardian times, a thyme lawn releases a beautiful fragrance when walked on and when in flower will create

Opposite: Nasturtiums always make a wonderful display.

a purple lavender carpet. It's drought-resistant, establishes quickly and is low-maintenance, requiring just a good shearing after flowering to keep it in shape.

Creeping thyme (*Thymus coccineus*) is, as its name suggests, a spreader. It has deep pink flowers and it's very popular with bees. *T. serpyllum* 'Elfin' is a compact variety that is highly suitable for creating lawns. Woolly thyme (*T. pseudolanuginosus*) has silvery-green leaves with a fast-spreading habit. A patchwork quilt effect looks great – achieve this by mixing up these varieties and planting around 15 centimetres apart. It can also be sensible to include a pathway if you have heavy foot-traffic through this area.

Clover

Clover lawns are another possibility. Clover is more drought-tolerant than grass, deliciously soft underfoot and a better option for dog owners who are struggling with pet urine stains on the lawn. If you already have clover in your lawn, you could also throw some seed down now to encourage more plants, and don't mow your lawn after they flower in summer so they can set seed and take over.

Clover is a nitrogen-fixing plant – this means it adds nitrogen to the soil, obviating the need for fertilizer – and it will smother most other weeds. It's very attractive to bees and on a warm summer's evening smells like honey.

Opposite, bottom left: Here the wild orchids and flowers are left in peace, yet the lawn is mown for access.
Opposite, top: At Trinity College Dublin the formal lawns have been replaced with a flowering meadow.
Opposite, bottom right: Daisies and buttercups are allowed to flourish in this lawn.

In praise of magnolias

Magnolias are among the oldest groups of flowering plants and have long been cultivated. The beautiful magnolias in our parks and gardens come from an ancient genus. Some fossilised specimens have been dated as far back as 20 million years. The wide-open flower shape evolved from the plant's requirement to be pollinated by beetles – magnolias pre-date the evolution of honey bees. The distinctive flower centres developed to become extremely tough to avoid being eaten by the pollinators themselves – a useful feature for any flower.

Magnolias can be witnessed in their full glory every spring at Caerhays Castle Gardens in Cornwall. This magnificent woodland garden is the home of a historic collection of Chinese plants that can be traced back to the great plant hunters of the late 1800s, including Ernest Wilson and George Forrest. As well as magnolia seeds, Caerhays took delivery of rhododendrons, camellias, azaleas and acers, and a huge number of these plants can be admired in their maturity today. Most fascinatingly, they also formed the basis of many new hybrids that grace our gardens today. When you see the magnolias blooming in this Cornish forest, they look as if they have always been there but they represent an amazing part of plant history. Unlike many non-native species, which can look out of place, these massive magnolias settled into their new landscape beautifully.

Approximately two-thirds of all known magnolia species are found in Asia, a large proportion of them in southern China. In the wild, magnolias act as indicators of the wellbeing of the forest in which they are found, but sadly almost half of all wild Chinese magnolias are at risk of extinction, so it has become necessary to start cataloguing the numbers that remain and restoring their surviving habitats in an effort to save them. The loss of more magnolia species would be catastrophic, not only for reasons of genetic diversity, but also because wild magnolias are a significant source of food, medicine and timber for local communities in China and across the Asian continent.

Opposite:
Magnolia × *Soulangeana* blooms against a crisp spring sky.

Types of magnolia

Most of the magnolias you will find in your local garden centre would have been brought into the country quite recently, but many would have been derived from the legendary Victorian plant excursions. The choice of magnolia for your garden will depend on the space you have available; they can grow to an enormous size and will outgrow an inadequate space quicker than you think.

Magnolia grandiflora

This is the most beautiful evergreen shrub with large, shiny grooved leaves that have a rusty sheen on their underside. Unlike most deciduous magnolias, it comes into flower in late summer to early autumn – and the wait is worthwhile. Its huge creamy-white cup-shaped flowers can be up to 25 centimetres in diameter.

New cultivars include M. *grandiflora* 'Ferruginea', which produces the most elegant pale cream blooms, and M. *grandiflora* 'Heaven Scent', which has richly scented flower petals that are pink on the outside and white on the inside.

Deep pink shades

Magnolias look great in deep pink shades; M. *liliiflora* 'Nigra' is a deciduous shrub with purple to pink goblet-shaped flowers in summer and M. *veitchii* 'Peter Veitch' has pure white flowers with a soft pink that bleeds gently into the flower from its base.

For smaller gardens

For the smaller garden, M. *stellata*, with its starry white flowers, is just stunning, as is M. 'Susan', with its large and reliable deep-purple flowers.

Deciduous magnolias

The magnificence of the deciduous magnolias is most evident in spring when their bare wooden skeletons are clothed in these dramatic flowers. Their growth habit is generally very open, with spreading branches that display the flowers to perfection. Bright green foliage bursts out soon after flowering to complete the annual life cycle of the perfect garden tree.

Opposite, top: *Magnolia* 'Leonard Messel'.
Opposite, bottom: A white *Magnolia stellata* shines in Bellefield Gardens.

May

May is an explosion. It's when summer begins, and plants are growing at an extraordinary rate. You run around trying to achieve the impossible, directing growth, mowing lawns and feeding and weeding – it feels like a never-ending task. But daylight is on your side and by the end of the month the long summer evenings confirm that summer is here. The old reliables come to the fore – lupins, aquilegia and a host of early-summer plants put on spectacular displays, and the green garden of April suddenly pops with colour. Hedgerows are full of the white flower of our native hawthorn, *Crataegus monogyna*. Along the roadside, the delicate, beautiful white flowers of cow parsley create the greatest garden.

May is the month of the Chelsea Flower Show, gardening's greatest event. At least one visit is a must. Whether it's the headlining show gardens that delight or the scents wafting from the colourful rose stands in the Great Marquee, a visit will take your breath away. Amazement can be found in the horticultural trickery that gets spring-flowering plants at their absolute peak mid-month. Growers use all their knowledge to have the plants that they devote their lives to looking their best. And for many that's what gardening is all about.

Opposite: Evening light in Paul's garden.

The Chelsea chop

The Chelsea chop is a technique you can practise in your own garden in late May – around the time of the great flower show. It's a way of cutting back herbaceous and perennial plants to make them bushier and to get them to flower slightly later. It can be good for plants that get leggy later in the year, such as *Nepeta*. (*Nepeta* is a good alternative to lavender, which struggles to grow well in wet conditions, especially over winter.) Chopping it in late May means that its growth will be checked, and the plant will throw out more shoots and flower later. This makes it less leggy and more bushy. The plant needs to be of a reasonable size – it's important not to chop too early in May if plants have only just reached the right growing stage – for example, if their growth was delayed by a chilly spring.

The technique involves pruning the plant back by about a third, which means reducing the plant stems. You can either chop the whole plant, or selected plants in the group, or individual stems on the plant.

Opposite: Hardy geraniums can be tricked into flowering later by chopping them now.

Weeding

PAUL

I tend to weed my garden twice a year. First, in late autumn or early spring, I clear last year's growth and remove every trace of weeds, including the roots of any pernicious perennial weeds. Some years I mulch the garden in spring with whatever I can get my hands on. Other years I stand back and let the plants grow.

From February through to November there is always something I've planted growing and flowering in the garden so there's very little space for the weeds to grow. In midsummer I wade in for a second weed. And if I'm feeling particularly vigilant, or if there's a gardening visitor popping by, I'll reluctantly do a another weed in the late summer.

We take a very lax approach to weeds. They are nothing more than plants in the wrong place. Some are persistent and fill us with dread, but most weeds, if kept in check, are easy to live with and many are food sources or a habitat for wildlife.

Pull your weeds before they set seed – one year's seeding is seven years' weeding! Your method of weeding may be simply deadheading and not removing the whole weed – this will make future weeding that little bit less daunting. Annual weeds such as bittercress, willowherb and chickweed are easy to eradicate by either pulling them up or hoeing them on a dry day and allowing them to wilt.

Other perennial weeds that can be an issue include those with long tap roots such as dandelion and dock. These ideally need pulling out with a fork, taking as much tap root as possible. Restricting them from seeding freely is the best method of control.

In a newly established garden you will rely heavily on mulch, and it is a good idea to be a little more vigilant with weeds for the first year or two as your plants mature and develop. Heavy mulching really is your friend here, along with planting densely and careful selection of plants.

We don't believe in using chemicals and try to garden as organically as possible. Many countries are banning the use of chemicals because they cause so much harm to both the environment and to ourselves, so for these reasons we try to avoid them. Even the best gardener gets it wrong sometimes, though, and both our gardens have problem areas where the weeds are winning the battle. Persistence and vigilance are the only ways you'll keep the weeds at bay; or, if you take our approach, cultivate an attitude of acceptance and don't rush out with the hoe too often. It's a far more relaxed approach that allows both the gardener and everything else that inhabits the space to thrive.

DIARMUID

I'm a lazy gardener. Most of the work in my garden during the growing season is simply admiration, with the occasional clearance of blocked paths. I do, however, draw the line at perennial weeds, such as bindweed, ground elder and scutch grass. They should be dug out, root and all – any bit of broken root left in the soil will regrow. Those three, along with mare's tail, are the real problem weeds in a garden because they really do take over if you allow them to.

Above left: A field of dandelion seedheads. Even weeds can be beautiful!
Left: White clover in a lawn.
Far left: An orchid in a lawn – a very welcome weed.

Bedding plants

Late May is usually a safe time to plant out bedding plants, but don't rush. If it's a cold May, the plants will not like it outside and being planted out when it is cold can cause them to sulk. The plants we buy from garden centres and online have been grown in perfect conditions – warm, no wind or cold and a perfect amount of water. Bringing these plants home and sticking them outside in cold weather and a chill wind will give them a shock and set back growth, perhaps for a number of weeks. It is always better to plant bedding plants during a warm spell and get them off to a good start.

Even if the plant is fully hardy, it is essential to harden off plants grown under glass to prepare them for being planted outside. To do this, put the plants outside on milder days and nights, gradually exposing them to more and more time in the outside conditions. On colder days and nights, bring them under glass or cover with a fleece, gradually reducing the cover until they are out 24/7 and acclimatised to the growing conditions outside.

If you have a potting shed or greenhouse it is a good idea to plant the containers with bedding earlier and grow them on in the greenhouse until late May. The plants will get established in the container and will be more mature when moved outside.

Whether your plants are outside or in, nip out the growing points to produce a bushier plant – otherwise some plants, particularly petunia, fuchsia and verbena, will grow leggy. Whether growing bedding plants inside, on windowsills or in the greenhouse, we usually stop them from flowering by pinching out the flowers until ready for planting out. There is no point in the plant using energy to flower in the greenhouse. Nip out the flower and divert the energy to the plant growth until outside in the garden.

Above: *Tagetes* 'Cinnabar' from Great Dixter (French marigold).
Opposite: White cosmos, *Agastache aurantiaca* 'Apricot Sprite' and a host of annuals fill these pots.

PAUL

I was once asked to turn up at a garden where the owner had arranged a delivery of plants to coincide with my visit. I was lured there under the false pretence of being invited for lunch, but the real reason for my trip soon became clear. The garden had been newly renovated, and the plants were the final touch. The owner had made the mistake of going to the garden centre the week before and picking out what they liked and looked good there and then. Technically there's nothing wrong with this, but no consideration had been given to the aspect, soil type or even the style of garden. The result was a mismatch of planting, with no clear thought process and some specimens that I felt weren't suited to the environment and would struggle.

Principles of planting

A planting scheme needs planning. Choose the right plant for the right place. There are plants for all situations; you just need to understand what your situation is and decide what you like that will suit it. Planting a new garden can be a very personal thing and you do need to consider what you do and don't like, as well as the overall style you want to achieve.

Things to consider

Colour
If you are all about colour you need to choose a broad palette of plants, with every colour of flower and foliage imaginable to create a picture-perfect cottage-garden style of planting.

Effect
Maybe you prefer the calming effect of plants, in which case you'll be far happier with large, lush greenery and some choice grasses – minimalist yet highly effective.

Quantity
A successful small garden can have as few as three different plants or as many as thirty. Personally, we could never cope in a garden with only three different plants, but we do appreciate a well-executed garden of this style.

Choosing your plants
To ensure year-round succession and flowers for every month, it's a good idea to visit your local garden centre every month of the year and return with a plant that's looking good on each visit. That way your garden will have an interesting plant for every season, even if you aren't sure what it is called!

When you're picking the ideal plants, it is always best to plant in odd numbers. Threes or fives or even sevens are ideal for creating clumps and drifts of grasses or perennials. This isn't always practical or feasible, however. Don't forget, one is an odd number too, and it's better to plant in ones than not at all. Lots of perennials increase in size with age and a single plant can be split and divided over time to colonise a much larger area.

Coverage is the whole aim of any planting we do. Weeds take up our time, and they steal nutrients and water from the plants we want. By planting more densely we can use the plants we like to suppress the weeds.

A well-thought-out planting plan should require very minimal maintenance apart from dealing with the odd weeds until the plants establish. Keep in mind that nature doesn't do bare soil, so if you insist on cultivating an area just to keep it weed free, you'll be pulling weeds for ever more. Plant something in that area and you'll only be weeding for as long as it takes for the desired plant to fill that position.

Paul's plant of the month

Holboellia brachyandra

This is a strange but wonderful climber that comes all the way from Vietnam. It's an evergreen twining climber with glossy green foliage. In 2018, the climber in my garden survived a battering from the 'beast from the east' with no issues. It flowers in May, around Chelsea week, and bears a profusion of off-white bell-shaped flowers, which are decorative and very attractive – but the main attraction is the scent. It smells of perfectly ripe melon, filling the air on those long balmy May evenings with the most magnificent scent. The flowers are followed in autumn by aubergine-like fruits, which are edible, albeit bland. Stories circulate that they are great roasted, but it's not something I've tried yet! It's best planted in pairs if you do want fruit.

Mulch!

Another way of dealing with weeds is mulching. If there was only one piece of advice we could give to gardeners it would be to mulch. Mulching is simple – it just means spreading a material on the surface of the soil. Compost or bark are best as they break down and ultimately add to soil quality, but you can mulch with stone too – it's particularly effective in a seaside garden. Mulch suppresses weeds, improves the soil structure and conserves moisture in the drier summer months. Mulching will help your plants to grow and make it extremely easy for you to pull out weeds for the first season or two as the plants develop. As long as you plant densely enough, by year three or four you shouldn't have too many problems with weeds smothering plants.

Lots of landscapers use membranes to cover the soil and suppress the weeds. In theory this is great, but in our experience as professionals it is not an effective solution. Many plants we want to grow spread their roots in the soil, which means that using a membrane straightaway stops them spreading, so instead of plants filling the gaps, weeds will. A bark mulch or gravel layer spread over a membrane may stop the weeds for a season or two, but weeds will prevail and make their way in, often growing in the mulch or gravel as it becomes a suitable place for seeds to germinate.

Restricting the spreading ability of plants in the area makes it become 'static', with only the large shrubs and trees really growing. In time the layer of bark rots down and the gravel gets mucky and thin, exposing the plastic. The soil below this membrane tends to get compacted and lacks air, as you are putting a layer of plastic over it. And the most annoying aspect is if you want to add new plants or even replace those that have died you have to struggle with a tangled mass of mucky, stinking plastic!

Choosing a few ground-covering plants, such as hardy geraniums like 'Patricia', or *Persicaria affinis* 'Darjeeling Red', is a far better long-term solution.

Opposite: This wild garden needs little maintenance.

Tree ferns

DIARMUID

For about ten years I travelled incessantly and moved house nearly as often. I was longing for the day when I could put down roots, set some seeds and plant tree ferns. Eventually it happened in the garden of our County Wicklow home. On the first terrace of my sloping site I built a rectangular pool and surrounded it with ten Dicksonia antarctica. A first-floor veranda at the back of the house acts as a perfect viewing platform to look down on them.

There's nothing recent about the popularity of tree ferns in Northern European gardens – they've been grown in gardens in these islands for over two hundred years. They were first introduced from Australia in 1786, when they were collected by plant hunters and sent back to London's botanical garden at Kew. Their introduction to gardens may have been accidental, however. Their trunks were used as ballast for cargoes during long sea journeys in the nineteenth century. When the ships were unloaded at the docks, some of the discarded trunks resprouted and were taken away to be replanted in gardens.

What was different in the early 2000s was their use in suburban gardens and their widespread availability not only in garden centres but also in DIY outlets that also had a trade in plants. There was an explosion of interest in these dramatic ferns and they became feature plants in our back gardens.

Where Diarmuid lives is not far from the coast, so it's generally warmish with only occasional snow. Tree ferns love airborne moisture and dance for joy at the sight of a heavy downpour. In the right conditions they grow fairly fast, and his collection are now sprouting fronds reminiscent of feathery ostrich plumes. They're lush, green and appear to be very happy.

What was just a few years ago a relatively bare terrace now looks like a subtropical jungle. Diarmuid has underplanted them with a wonderful shade-loving perennial, *Geranium palmatum*, and that results in a cloud of pink froth weaving its way around the base of the dark, hairy stems. As a combination it's a real delight, and even on the dullest days the drama of this plantation lifts the heart. Diarmuid doesn't cut off the dead fronds – he likes the layers of colour with fresh lime-green on top and bronzy leaves underneath. It replicates what happens in nature and prevents the tree ferns looking overly neat. Water the stem and crown because that's where the roots are.

Above left: Tree ferns used in Diarmuid's garden.
Above right: Tree ferns are used here with bananas for a tropical feel.
Left: Fronds unfurling!
Over: Tree ferns around Diarmuid's veranda.

Staking plants

May is the right time to stake perennials. Staking plants has a number of purposes. It supports stems to protect them from damage, especially wind damage. Also, it enables you to train the plant, stopping it flopping over and keeping it upright so that it doesn't lie on top of or swamp neighbouring plants. Some more vigorous perennials can grow over their neighbours and smother them. So staking helps to keep plants in order, but it is important to get the stakes in place early. It is so easy to leave this job until it's too late. Staking and putting supports around plants, particularly herbaceous perennials, helps them to look their best when in full bloom later in the year, but it becomes more difficult to insert the stake as the plant puts on more leaf. If the plant is more mature, it is tricky to get the support in place without damaging plants or the budding flower heads.

Many plants need support – for example, delphiniums, dahlias, alliums; anything that waves around in the wind looking vulnerable or that has heavy plant heads, such as peonies and oriental poppies. The choice of support depends on the type of plant. For example, peonies do well with a grid support, delphiniums are better suited to individual stakes, and plants such as crocosmia respond best to firm supports that keep the plant upright, with string or raffia linking the supports. Make sure any ties you use are soft and that there is room for the plant to grow.

Opposite: Although they are tall, these salvias, eryngiums and astrantias all support themselves, thanks to being densely planted.

June

If May is an explosion, June is insane. There's a kaleidoscope of colour and everything seems to be in bloom at once. You often have to wade your way through the garden to get into it, and as fast as the plants grow, so do the weeds.

Expect heatwaves and deluges of rain in equal measure. If the garden is half-decent it's like a lotto win – what you've achieved by doing so little is incomprehensible to you. It's the cheat's month; everything looks wonderful and bare soil disappears under lushness.

Opposite: Diarmuid's garden bursts into life in early summer.

Biennials

We associate spring with sowing seeds, especially annuals –
those plants that germinate, flower and die all in the same year.
However, there is another category of plant – biennials – that can
be sown from early to midsummer. Biennials take two years to
complete their life cycle. Sow them now and they will germinate
and form a rosette of leaves this year, which will be followed by a
spike of flowers next spring. The plant will then set seed and die
off in the autumn and winter.

Many of our best-loved flowers are in this category – foxgloves,
forget-me-not, Queen Anne's lace (cow parsley), sweet Williams
and wallflowers. So, if you'd like to see these in your garden next
year, harvest or buy some seed now and get propagating. You
won't get the instant gratification that annuals provide, but with a
little patience and dedication you will be rewarded with colourful
and often fragrant flowers that both you and our friendly bees and
butterflies will enjoy. They can be added to pots or containers or
simply used to fill gaps in the garden. They all tend to flower early
in the season, a time gardeners sometimes call the hungry gap
between spring and summer, so they can be an extremely useful
addition to the garden.

Opposite, top left: *Digitalis purpurea* – foxglove.
Opposite, top right: Echiums are giant biennials!
Opposite, bottom right: Forget-me-nots are a classic biennial.
Opposite, bottom left: Echium flowers.

Companion planting

Companion planting is not a new concept; it has been practised for hundreds, if not thousands, of years. When American colonists took over native American villages three hundred years ago the most observant noticed something about how they were growing their crops. In Europe most crops were planted in straight rows, but the native Americans had what at first seemed a messy way of growing their sweetcorn, climbing beans and pumpkins. First, sweetcorn is planted and allowed to grow upright. At the base of the sweetcorn a climbing bean is added and, finally, beneath the two a pumpkin or courgette is grown. Oddly, this works remarkably well, all three crops benefiting each other. The sweetcorn provides support for the bean, the bean is a legume so it fixes nitrogen, and the pumpkin creates ground cover and shade to keep the others' roots cool and prevent water loss. This method is known as the three sisters and is a great example of how plants can be grown in harmony with each other to benefit both the crops and the gardener.

Opposite, top left: Calendula is often used as a companion plant.
Opposite, top right and bottom left: Lavender attracts a host of beneficial insects.
Opposite, bottom right: Calendula is used as a companion plant in lavender fields.
Over: A field of lavender in Somerset.

Favourite companion plants

A favourite plant combination is growing nasturtiums to deter aphids or alliums to ward off carrot root fly. Some plants can be grown as a sacrificial plant – if grown alongside beans, aphids will attack them and not your crop! As a general rule companion plants have a strong scent, which attracts pests to them and away from others they might otherwise attack.

Mint

Mint is an all-rounder companion plant, keeping pests of lots of common veg crops at bay, but don't plant it in the ground because it's a thuggish spreader! Grow it in pots around the garden.

Lavender

Due to its strong scent lavender attracts lots of beneficial pollinators as well as deterring aphids. Grown as a hedge in a veg garden it can be productive and beautiful.

Pot marigold

Pot marigold (*Calendula officinalis*) helps repel whitefly from tomatoes and lure aphids off beans. It also attracts beneficial insects such as ladybirds, lacewings and hoverflies, which prey on aphids.

Roses

Roses are central to our vision of a country garden, at the heart of which is a cottage covered in roses. A favourite garden image is a rambling rose that has scrambled up an old tree and brought it new life with a crown of flowers. It's amazing how many places you come across roses being grown – they're even found in nurseries at the base of the Atlas Mountains in Morocco, crammed with the plant that we all think the epitome of the gardens on these islands.

People have been adoring this royal genus among plants for millennia, and the rose symbolises love and friendship. When the 49 delegates to the inaugural conference of the United Nations assembled in San Francisco on 22 June 1945, a few days before they signed the UN Charter, they each found a 'Peace' rose in their hotel room with a card from the American Rose Society that read, 'This is the Peace rose, christened in Pasadena on the day Berlin fell. We hope the Peace rose will influence men's thoughts for everlasting world peace.'

They are a wonderfully versatile plant – they can be a shrub, climber, rambler, specimen, ground cover or even miniature, so there is probably space in your garden for at least one – even in a tub. For excellent value you can buy bare-root roses in the winter, any time between November and March. Container-grown roses are suitable for planting year-round, though the choice tends to be a little narrower.

There's a specific issue when it comes to planting roses to be aware of. If you plant a rose where they have grown before you'll find that the new plant won't thrive and may even die. This is due to rose replant disease, a strange quirk of the species. You can plant them in a different area or, if you have no option, you can grow a covering of corn marigolds for a year or two. They seem to sterilise the soil of whatever residue the old roses leave and allow the new roses to grow happily.

When planting, pick the best spot you can – sunny, airy, sheltered and with really good soil. Improve your soil by adding plenty of well-rotted manure or compost. If planting a climber, plant at least a foot away from the wall to avoid dryness around the root system. They can also be planted among herbaceous plants to create a more naturalistic environment where pests and diseases are less likely to thrive. But one of the best ways of ensuring problem-free roses is to choose varieties that have been bred to be highly resistant, such as the perennial favourites 'Gertrude Jekyll' and 'Iceberg'.

The range of roses available is vast, so when you're visiting other gardens it's a good idea to have a handy notebook to jot down your favourites. Catalogues are wonderfully informative, but they can't tell you how the plant actually smells, and it is the delicious perfume that often makes us fall in love with a particular species.

Shrub roses

To pick favourites in such a huge pool of great plants is hard, but here are a few shrub roses we enjoy:

Rosa 'Bengal Crimson'

This is a real gem. It has single flowers, so it's much more closely related to its wild cousins than all the highly bred roses we are used to, but with the most intense rich scarlet flowers. It has a very lax habit, so is best grown with some support. Its real charm is that it can flower nearly all through winter in a mild year.

Rosa 'Rhapsody in Blue'

Blue is the rarest colour in the garden and the name in this case is a little misleading. It is more a soft purple, with a white centre. It's a shrub rose and useful in any mixed planting – a plant that has thrived for years in Paul's garden with nothing but neglect.

Rosa 'Olivia Rose Austin'

World-renowned plantswoman Helen Dillon once told us that if a rose breeder names a plant for one of the family members it must be a good one. She was right. This is a David Austin rose with a gorgeous double pink flower that is wonderfully scented. The flowers are large, first appearing in early June and repeating all summer. It's vigorous, forms a healthy shrub and is just an all-round good doer.

Ramblers and climbers

DIARMUID

Rosa 'Lady Hillingdon' is a climbing rose recommended by Helen Dillon. According to Helen, she's terrible in bed but just brilliant against a wall! And indeed this apricot lady's blossoms are made up of large petals, resulting in long, elegant, waxy buds that open to large, loosely formed flowers. These hang gracefully from the branches and emit a delicious, rich tea fragrance. She repeats flowers throughout the summer and is exhausted by autumn.

Climbing roses tend to be less vigorous than ramblers and more manageable for a smaller garden. Our favourite climber has to be *Rosa* 'Gertrude Jekyll', a bright pink double David Austin rose with the most amazing scent. It flowers early and is a reliable repeat flowerer. David Austin roses combine the best of the old roses, such as scent and colour, while also being disease-resistant and able to cope with a degree of neglect.

Rambling roses are different from climbing roses. Unlike climbers, which often repeat bloom in late summer, ramblers generally only flower once, usually in May or June. The flowers are normally smaller than climbers' flowers, but as they hang together in big trusses or clusters the overall effect is dramatic. As they only flower once, all their energy goes into this dazzling display. It also means that there's no requirement to deadhead, so you just leave the blossoms on to form rose hips in autumn.

The other major difference is their flexible canes. Their pliability allows you to train them around pergolas, arbours and arches or fan out the canes to spread over a wall. But beware – they can be extremely vigorous, behaving like fast-growing vines and smothering their supports.

A wonderful oddity

The largest rose in the world is a rambler that extends to 465 square metres (5,000 square feet). It was planted by Scottish settlers in 1885 in Tombstone, Arizona. A woman was homesick and when sent a bunch of bulbs and cuttings from her home country she set about planting them around the coach house they were staying in. One was a rooted cutting of Lady Banks' Rose. As the rose grew, a pergola was built from poles and trellis to support it. It is still blooming today, and the town holds an annual Rose Festival for rose lovers around the world to come and enjoy the spectacle.

Rosa 'American Pillar'

This is a rambling rose that you really need space for. It has single bright pink flowers with white centres and will quickly cover a wall or any other structure you allow it to ramble though. It does only flower once but is fairly tough and doesn't seem to suffer too much from any of the common rose ailments

Opposite: Rosa 'Gertrude Jekyll'.

Rosa banksiae – **Lady Banks' Rose**

Wearing masses of white fragrant flowers and often described as violet scented, it's unusual as it flowers early in the year, usually around April and May, and it's thornless. There's a beautiful yellow version – 'Lutea' – but only if you have adequate space!

Roses for a tree

If you want to create the classic look of a rose growing through an old tree, we would recommend a fairly vigorous climber such as 'Paul's Himalayan Musk'. It tolerates poor soil and a bit of shade and bears delightfully musky scented dainty pink blush roses. A bare-root rose will establish more quickly, so this is a project for the next month or so. Dig a planting hole around a metre in distance from the tree trunk – you want to avoid damaging the tree's root system. Add compost to the planting hole and position your rose at an angle leaning towards the tree. Put in a cane that will extend to the trunk of the tree to support the plant on its journey, firm the soil and water in.

However, there are gentler cultivars available, such as 'Super Fairy', which has clusters of small pink double flowers and reaches about 3 metres in height, making it a good option for a trellis or small archway. 'Rambling Rosie' is another short one, this time with crimson flowers, and 'Goldfinch' has the benefit of being nearly thornless and carries lovely primrose-yellow flowers.

Opposite, top left: A classic rose: *Rosa rugosa*.
Opposite, top right: *Rosa* 'American Pillar'.
Opposite, bottom: *Rosa* 'Perennial Blue'.

Herb gardens

Why not grow your own crop of fresh herbs to enhance your cooking? Summer is the best time to enjoy them fresh from the garden. And they're often very easy to grow!

Many of the most familiar and most versatile herbs are indigenous to the Mediterranean where they grow in quite poor conditions: dry soils with very little water. This means that herbs such as rosemary, oregano and thyme are easy to grow; they'll thrive without much care and attention. Moreover, each time you take a little bit from the plant for the kitchen, you are effectively pinching it out, which encourages more and bushier growth.

Pots, large planters and window boxes are more than capable of supporting a fantastic herb garden. Herbs will even flourish in hanging baskets and you can plant them among other flowering perennials or edible plants such as nasturtiums, calendulas and pansies to create something gorgeous. Along with adding a spark to your food, herbs are really beautiful plants in their own right and will complement most ornamentals in a flower border.

Make sure that you give them the best possible start with fertile, well-drained compost, and position them in good light. A small amount of extra drainage – sand or grit – will benefit lavender, rosemary and tarragon. Herbs do like the soil to be quite dry, but avoid letting it dry out completely as rewetting the compost can be difficult. Soak the whole container in a bucket of water if need be.

Here's our choice of easy herbs to grow.

Mint (*Mentha* spp.)

It's invasive, but if you keep it in a pot or even submerged in a pot underground you can control it. It likes moisture and rich soil. Did you know you can grow chocolate-flavoured mint (*M. × piperata* 'Chocolate') and even strawberry mint (*M. spicata* subsp. *citrata* 'Strawberry')? They make lovely herbal teas or additions to summer cocktails. Mint grows well from cuttings, including root cuttings.

Sage (*Salvia officinalis*)

Sage has softly textured foliage with mauve flower spikes, and the purple-leaved cultivar is particularly impressive. It is an essential in many Italian dishes and is great for flavouring olive oil. Grow in well-drained soil and hard-prune in spring to promote a bushy habit.

Fennel (*Foeniculum vulgare*)

Fennel is a real favourite in contemporary vegetable gardens as, apart from its culinary use, it has soft feathery foliage that provides texture and architectural shape to the edible garden. You could grow the bronze version, 'Purpureum', in a herbaceous border – its seed heads will look good right into winter.

Basil (*Ocimum basilicum*)

Basil is a must; it has the freshest green colour and a wafting fragrance that will fill the air around the patio. It is tender – it will vanish if you plant it out too early – and it can be quick to bolt if it's overcrowded or dries out. Best grown from seed in April and planted out in June. Bring it in for the winter and put it on your kitchen windowsill.

Rosemary (*Rosmarinus officinalis*)

Rosemary will thrive anywhere. As it's evergreen it can be placed in and around herbaceous species that die down over winter so that a green skeleton will remain all year round.

Chives (*Allium schoenoprasum*)

Chives come up fresh every year. Their strong grass-like foliage provides a great contrast with other herbs, and the pink flowers make an attractive garnish in salads. It likes a rich, well-drained soil. Divide the clumps every few years.

Sweet cicely (*Myrrhis odorata*)

If you're looking to cut down on sugar, this herb is a natural sweetener. Crushing the leaves produces a liquorice scent – delicious! It's also a very pretty plant for the herbaceous border, with umbels of white flowers and ferny foliage.

Bay laurel (*Laurus nobilis*)

Bay looks fantastic when grown alone in patio pots and can be shaped into lollipops, pyramids or large balls. It offers a smart and formal touch to an outdoor living space and will flavour food dishes from Indian curries to the traditional roast dinner. Collect leaves for drying in summer. Tolerates some shade.

July

On Instagram, every garden appears glorious and every gardening magazine and television show is packed with beautiful blossoms, and people are using their spaces in the most photogenic ways. If you were to take all this to heart, you'd think that if your garden isn't perfect by now, you've missed the bus, and if your garden isn't brilliant, beautiful, lovely or even okay, give up. Mow the grass and start planning in October.

But this is the month to actually sit out and use your garden, whatever it looks like. Just enjoy what you have – if you're not planning any changes this month. Use your garden as another room. If it makes you feel any better, remember that a lot of the Instagrammers are putting an awful lot of effort into making each photo perfect. It takes them hours to get the best shots, and they never show the bad ones. And the photographers arrive at 4.45 a.m. to set up the idyllic images that will appear in the garden magazines.

Opposite: *Echinops* and *Macleaya* in summer evening light.

Creating a wildflower meadow

The simple act of letting your lawn grow will create a meadow. To some, this is just an unkempt landscape. But when meadow grasses are allowed to flower you begin the process of creating a wildflower meadow. It may not be the colourful masterpiece that we associate with the term 'wildflower meadow', but it will be just as beneficial to our ecosystem. By allowing your lawn to grow and only cutting it a few times a year you will create a humble but functional meadow, full of pollen for creatures like moths. You might also be surprised to see what pops up among the grass. You'd probably expect daisies, clover, dandelions, speedwell and buttercup, but depending on your soil type, you could also spot orchids, cowslips, oxeye daisies or harebells.

In general, grass dominates and tends to elbow out wildflowers. To encourage flowers that you like, you may need to reduce the grasses' vigour by introducing semi-parasitic plants such as yellow rattle (*Rhinanthus minor*) and eyebright (*Euphrasia* spp.). Scatter their seed in late summer and autumn on short grass.

If you really want a flower-filled meadow you will have to put in some extra effort and reseed the whole area using an appropriate mix. You can also introduce flowers by planting plug plants.

Looking at any blank canvas can be daunting, but the process is relatively simple, and once it's established a meadow will drastically reduce the work you need to do in your garden.

Opposite: Paul's wildflower meadow garden.

Planning your meadow

Area

Examine the area you want to turn into a meadow. Is it sunny all day? What's the soil like? What has the area been used for in the past? The light a site receives is important as most of our native wildflowers require sun for most of the day. If the area is in shade for more than half of the day during the summer, you'll need to consider using a special mix for shady areas.

Soil

The soil is the next important consideration. Wildflowers thrived in meadows of old, which were cut later in the season and weren't improved with any artificial fertilizers. So the best thing to do with your soil is nothing! Poorer soils suit wildflowers, so improving your soil by adding fertilizer will be detrimental to the success of a meadow. And as annual growth of grass and flowers dies away in autumn it's important to remove the organic material to reduce the amount of nutrients returning to the soil.

What to plant

The most important consideration is what you want the area to do. Are you interested in attracting as many pollinators as possible and happy to designate an area to simply become a wildflower patch?

An area like this will provide months of interest in the summer and, most important, will be a rich food source for pollinators. Perhaps you have an area by the road you don't fancy cutting all the time? In this case you could pick a low-flowering mix. This will give you a beautiful, low-maintenance patch that won't be judged by passers-by, yet can still be cut, albeit a lot more infrequently than a grass lawn.

Or maybe you're just not sure what to put in your new garden and want to trial areas for borders.

Opposite, top: A meadow where areas of grass have just been left to grow.
Opposite, middle: Allowing grass to grow encourages wild orchids and other gems.
Opposite, bottom: *Phacelia tanacetifolia* used as part of an annual mix on a Dublin roundabout.
Above: An annual pollinator mix on a busy road.

Putting down an annual meadow mix will fill the garden with colour and give you time to think about how to develop your garden going forward.

How to do it

Hire a turf stripper for the day to lift the existing turf. You can then remove this and prepare the soil below, removing any large stones as well as perennial weeds. Prepping the ground for wildflower mixes is like preparing the ground for a normal lawn. Fork over or rotavate the soil, then firm the area by walking on it. Use a rake to level out the soil, which is now ready for seeding.

Don't work soil that's wet or waterlogged because it damages its structure and makes it difficult for the seeds when they first germinate. Don't worry about the inevitable weeds – as long as one doesn't entirely dominate, they will just add to the diversity of the meadow.

What next?

Keep the meadow long all summer and delay mowing until September to give time for the wildflowers to set seed. When you do mow, remove the clippings as otherwise they rot down and over-fertilise the soil, which will favour grasses over flowers. It will take a couple of years to get the balance right and it may need tweaking by adding seeds in spring.

DIARMUID

A number of different bird species have decided to make our home their home. We enjoy sharing our plot with robins, blue tits, great tits, blackbirds, goldfinches and chaffinches. I've been undertaking a few projects that will help keep them here, starting with creating spaces for some of them to nest and feed. During a visit to wildlife expert Ken Thompson's suburban Sheffield plot, where our voices were almost drowned out by a symphony of birdsong, I took notes on creating beneficial habitats for the birds. And I started by replacing wooden fences with hedges of beech and holly.

Wildlife gardening

With the growth of intensive farming our gardens are becoming increasingly important as nature reserves. Fields have become bigger, with the result that hedgerows are disappearing. When they're removed, much of the shelter and food that wildlife uses goes too. Simply changing the way we garden and taking a few steps to encourage wildlife will make our gardens of great benefit to a healthier ecosystem.

If we provide plants that attract wildlife it means that all sorts of creatures will be invited to the garden and an ecosystem will develop. Bugs and slugs we don't like will be eaten by the birds, beneficial predators of common garden pests will make our gardens their homes and we will rely less on chemical intervention to solve our gardening problems.

Even a small pool of water in the garden will create a wonderful amenity for us and other creatures. Placing some aquatic plants in a half-barrel works wonders. Try *Equisetum* for dramatic structure alongside a striped aquatic sedge. Starwort will help oxygenate the water, and finally you could add a dwarf water lily such as 'Ruby'. Aquatic plants can be vigorous growers, so keep everything in pots.

An arrangement of stones peeping out of the water will enable birds to land and have a drink or bathe. Dragonflies will lay their larvae in the water; the larvae will creep up the stems of the *Equisetum* and almost instantly a whole water ecosystem will develop. If the water clouds up a little bit through algae, add some barley extract, available from garden centres.

Opposite: A ladybird in bamboo.

Bog gardens

If you have a damp, poorly drained area, don't panic. People often consider this a problem because they feel that little likes to grow in wet soil. They might feel that they should immediately install drainage systems to enable the normal trees and shrubs we see in everyday gardens to thrive.

However, there are loads of plants that thrive with their feet in water, so you can make a virtue out of a waterlogged area by planting with lush plants that are happy in the damp. If you want evidence of this, you could do worse than to visit Mount Usher Gardens in Ashford, County Wicklow. It is situated on the banks of the River Vartry, so much of the soil is wet, but they have used the conditions to their advantage.

The best approach to deal with a damper garden is going along with it; work with what you are given rather than trying to dry out the land.

Ferns

There is a great range of ferns that love a moist soil, such as *Dryopteris filix-mas*, the male fern, with its beautiful shuttlecock-like tufts of fresh green fronds, *Osmunda regalis*, the royal fern, which turns reddish-brown in autumn, and *Athyrium filix-femina*, the lady fern, with its delicate lacy fronds. If you take care to regularly mist the fronds of *Dicksonia* ferns you will see how wonderfully they respond to a soaking not just in the ground but along their trunk and foliage.

Waterside plants

Many waterside plants have wonderful architectural leaves, the best-known being *Gunnera manicata*, giant rhubarb, but this can be invasive and grows enormous, so you do need adequate space to

Opposite: Timber paths in a bog garden.

grow it. As an alternative, try *Rheum palmatum* 'Atrosanguineum', an ornamental variety of rhubarb that has wonderful purple leaves that mature to green and produces spikes of flowers, or *Darmera peltata*, the umbrella plant, a vigorous clump-forming perennial which throws up clusters of pretty pale-pink flowers on naked stems in spring, followed by rhubarb-like leaves that go red in the autumn.

Good combinations with these on poor-draining, moist soil would be astilbes with their fluffy spikes of white, pink, purple or red flowers, ligularias for a splash of bright daisy-like flowers and large heart-shaped leaves, and *Aruncus dioicus*, or goat's beard, which has arching plumes of tiny creamy-white flowers. For primrose lovers, this is a great opportunity to plant candelabra primroses, those wonderful species which have tiers of flowers growing up the stem, such as the yellow/orange-flowered Bulley's primrose (*Primula bulleyana*) or the dark pink of the Japanese primrose (*P. japonica*). Vial's primrose (*P. vialii*) is perhaps the most striking; it looks like a cross between a primrose and a red hot poker, with cones of red-tipped lilac pink flowers. A native of China, found growing wild in wet meadows, this will be very happy beside a pond or lake.

There are some plants that don't like constant water but do well with a regular helping of it, such as bamboos. They grow beautifully by the edge of many a lake as they are quite thirsty.

The iris family

Finally we have to mention irises. The yellow flag, *Iris pseudacorus*, grows wild in bogs and is happy with its feet completely in water, so it's a true bog plants. But for areas that are just damp, how about the dramatic black-flowered *I. chryosgraphes* or, another favourite, *I. laevigata* 'Variegata', which has purple flowers and cream-striped foliage.

Above: Easter lily or *Zantedeschia* loves having damp feet.
Left: Rodgersia loves a damp garden.

Our favourite perennials

Perennials give great value in the garden, often performing for months and requiring little input. We've put together a few of our absolute favourites that will be happy in any garden.

Sedum spectabile 'Autumn Joy'

This plant has fleshy leaves and grows to 60 centimetres. In autumn it has large heads of pink flowers, which eventually fade to a coppery colour and then turn red. So don't cut them back until the spring to get the most interest from this plant.

Iris unguicularis (Algerian iris)

This is a winter-flowering evergreen iris that has lilac flowers from October to March. It reaches a height of 22 centimetres.

Hellebores

This genus has tons of choices that are hardy. The Christmas rose is popular for its midwinter white flowers, often appearing in the snow. Others have flowers in shades of green, red and purple. Awesome for winter interest, it has great foliage and flowers.

Hemerocallis (daylilies)

Daylilies are so called because each flower lasts only a single day, but the plants flower for weeks on end in the summer and are really tough, reliable plants that come in a remarkable range of colours.

Kniphofia (red hot poker)

The Popsicles series is a new selection of varieties that repeat flower over a long period of time and have colours from lime-green through to reds, oranges and yellows. 'Pineapple Popsicle' is a particularly elegant variety.

Hostas

Hostas have a long season of foliage interest and they can have attractive flowers too. Their very tough crowns make it hard for other plants to outcompete them. You need to keep the slugs and snails away, though.

Opposite: A perennial bed bursting with colour.

Campanulas

Campanula portenschlagiana is a lovely small ground hugger. For a larger plant, the enthusiastic self-seeder *C. persicifolia* is a great reliable cottage-garden perennial.

Nepeta (catmint)

Catmints are perfect for cottage-tyle gardens. *Nepeta* 'Six Hills Giant' is fairly tall; 'Walker's Low' is a good choice if you want a smaller one.

Dicentra (bleeding heart)

Dicentra 'Luxuriant' is particularly useful for shadier bits.

Hardy geraniums

Geranium 'Rozanne' is by far the longest-flowering variety. It's well worth growing.

Sanguisorbas

Underused perennials, they are great architectural plants that do very well, especially among grasses. They come in a huge variety of shapes and sizes for every situation.

Phlox paniculata

One of our favourite perennials for extending the season, they are vigorous, need little attention and come in a huge choice of colours.

Right and opposite: A selection of our favourite perennials.

Planting on a slope

As gardeners and landscape designers we are constantly faced with challenging situations. One of the most commons scenarios is a sloping bed or border that needs planting. The real issue is how to deal with this slope. We don't live in the Netherlands, so we have lots of slopes, and we tend to feel that conquering them with plants can be challenging. But it's really not that difficult. Making the correct choices is the trick.

First, take the opportunity to condition the soil – get some goodness back into it by introducing some organic material such as compost from your heap or well-rotted horse manure.

If you want a low-maintenance garden, it's good to be realistic about how much spare time you have to do gardening, but there's no such thing as zero maintenance. If it's not your hobby, you probably want easy plants and preferably no need to weed. However, you want it to look good with some colour at some stage in the year.

Planting on a slope brings its own complications. If you want a 'mini-terrace' you'll have to be mindful of planting so that the plant is standing straight up, not sticking out at an angle. The advantage of a slope is that it displays the plants very well, in a much more interesting way than a flat site.

Single species

If your site is in an open, sunny position you could choose a single species such as a bank of lavender – this will require an annual clip when the flowers are spent, but you will be rewarded with a glorious swathe of lavender-blue flowers and scent in the summer. Intersperse them with ground-cover hardy geraniums, such as 'Rozanne', that provide lots of flowers throughout the summer period.

Vincas

Vincas (periwinkles) do a great job of knitting the soil together as they creep along and there are some lovely bloomers, such as *Vinca minor* 'Bowles's Variety', which will act as a great weed suppressant.

Flower carpet roses

Flower carpet roses are very vigorous and prolific bloomers, and you can choose from pinks, reds and yellows. They have been bred to do the job of carpeting an area and are disease-resistant. They will require an annual trim and feed, but that's about it. Carpet roses are readily available in pots year-round. They can also be purchased in the bare-root season, which is any time from October to March; this is the cheapest way of planting a lot of roses.

Ornamental grasses

If you prefer a naturalistic look, you could plant a mixture of ornamental grasses, which provide a long season of interest and can look very attractive in winter. These only need cutting back in spring, but they will need to be divided to keep the planting fresh as the years progress. A good mix would be some tall *Stipa gigantea*, *Imperata cylindrica* 'Rubra' with its ruby-red tips, *Calamagrostris* 'Karl Foerster', *Molinia* and *Hakonechloa*.

Paul's plant of the month

Phlox

I find phlox invaluable in any garden. It's just a fantastic plant. We have a free-draining sandy soil that is very prone to drying out in summer, and late-summer interest can be difficult, if not impossible, in some years. Often the only plants that shine through are the various *Phlox paniculata* that I've accumulated. I can't name them as they've all been given as presents or divisions from other gardens, so often I'll name them according to who gave them to me. They are often criticised for suffering from powdery mildew, an issue in drier soils, but I don't mind the bit they get, and it has never affected the flowering for me. There are lots of new varieties and colours, and some are mildew-resistant ('Glamour Girl' being one).

August

In August it all collapses. August is fiery, it's a very intense month for colour, and it's the month when you lose the garden, no matter how good the planning you think you've done. Unless you're Christopher Lloyd, you lose the plot. A dry week or two in August can really mean the end of that beautiful garden as you know it. Anyway, you're in Benidorm or, if you're from Dublin's southside, Quinta do Lago – so do you really care?

Opposite: Diarmuid admiring a hydrangea walk in Co. Kerry.
Right: Some pots under the veranda in August.

Hydrangeas

DIARMUID

My favourite garden in America is an unusual one. Lombard Street in San Francisco is so steep that it has eight hairpin turns. The result is that motorists driving down the one-way street drive through a garden planted primarily with hydrangeas. All through the summer it delights residents and tourists with a bright display of shrubby flowers behind curved, sloping box borders.

Opposite: Blue *Hydrangea macrophylla* growing as a hedge.

What is it about hydrangeas? On our nightly Instagram broadcast they have been the most talked-about plant and they continue to be. We just love them! They are remarkably easy to grow, flower for a long time and thrive in our fairly cool, damp climate. For flower power it's hard to beat hydrangeas and although they're sometimes labelled old-fashioned, it's clear why they are so well loved.

Hydrangeas hail from south and eastern Asia (Japan, China, the Himalayas and Korea) and the Americas and were first introduced to these islands in the eighteenth century. The name hydrangea comes from the Greek word for water vessel – which is a good way of remembering that they don't like to get too dry.

Ideally, plant in moist, well-drained soil and in dappled shade – avoid dry sunny places. A bit of shelter is good, especially from biting cold easterly winds that can damage flower buds. That said, they're excellent maritime plants, having good tolerance to salty spray.

The Portuguese island of Faial in the Azores is also known as the Blue Island due to the abundance of blue hydrangeas growing there. Many a gardener has been disappointed after planting a beautiful blue hydrangea that then starts to produce pink flowers the following year. This is because the aluminium sulphate which makes the petals blue is only available for uptake by the plant in acidic soil.

If you don't have the right soil, the best way to ensure ideal conditions is to grow your hydrangea in a container so that you can control the pH of the soil by using special acidic compost and occasionally topping up with aluminium sulphate, sometimes known as hydrangea blueing compound.

While hydrangeas do quite well on neglect, they can become a bit leggy if left unpruned. It's not unusual to see small front gardens dominated by a hydrangea that has been left to its own

devices. Mophead and lacecap hydrangeas, the most commonly planted kind, will usually only require their old flower heads to be removed, cutting back to a pair of healthy buds. It's generally wise to leave this until spring as the old flower heads will give the more tender buds some protection from winter frosts. To keep the plant producing fresh stems, remove two or three older stems completely. If you have to chop back to return the plant to a manageable size, you will forfeit the flowers that year but they'll return the following year. Most hydrangeas flower on growth made the previous year.

H. arborescens 'Annabelle'

Everyone loves 'Annabelle' with her large domes of white flowers.

H. paniculata 'Vanilla Fraise'

We also love 'Vanilla Fraise', a paniculata hydrangea with cones of white flowers that age to a strawberry pink. Both paniculata and arborescent types flower on growth made in the season, so they can be pruned hard in spring and still flower later that summer.

H. aspera 'Macrophylla'

This will grow into a large shrub with big felty leaves and beautiful lacecap flowers, pure white on the outside surrounding a mauve centre. A real beauty.

H. petiolaris (climbing hydrangea)

And finally, don't forget the climbing hydrangea, H. petiolaris. It will happily grow up a north- or east-facing wall and, best of all, it doesn't need any supports like trellis or wire as it is self-supporting, clinging to the walls with its aerial roots. Like a lot of climbers, it can take a few years to really settle into a new home, but be patient – lots of growth will be happening underground as the plant spreads its roots and prepares to climb skywards.

Right: *Hydrangea macrophylla.*
Opposite, top: Hydrangeas and fuchsias in a cottage garden.
Opposite, bottom right: *Hydrangea paniculata.*
Opposite, bottom left: Lacecap hydrangea.
Over: A hydrangea in Diarmuid's garden.

Drought

We have to get used to the fact that we will soon be required to garden in a different way, planting for drought conditions and making every effort to conserve water. Our climate is changing. Look back over the weather patterns for the past fifty years and this becomes apparent. Every few years we have official droughts and hosepipe bans and our winters have become milder and more sporadic, with some very warm winters and the occasional deep freezes.

It can be hard to understand the science of it. We are surrounded by water, sea levels are rising, some islands in the Pacific will disappear under water, yet we sometimes don't have enough. As gardeners we will have to adapt, to change the way we garden. We will collect and store water. We will plant species that are moderate drinkers and plants such as cacti and succulents that can store water, and we will look for any other way to improve our gardening techniques that will enable our plots to flourish. The obvious plants to choose are ones that don't need a huge amount of water, so anything with furry, silvery leaves, such as stachys, verbascum and salvias, and Mediterranean species such as rosemary, thyme and lavender. Plants with succulent leaves, such as *Sedum spectabile*, waxy leaves like pittosporum, and spiky acanthus and eryngium are good choices too.

Beth Chatto's Gardens in Essex includes a gravel garden that is never watered. It uses only the meagre amount of rain that falls in that part of eastern England. The planting here is not typical of what you may imagine when dreaming of a country cottage garden, but the plants all do well with little rain, and we may be looking to use the same ideas here in the future.

Improved soil culture is essential for water retention. Make your own compost, and when you are planting, put a bucketful of good humus material around the roots. This will act like a capillary bed, clothing the roots in damper compost, which sucks up all the

moisture when added and makes it easy and freely available to those tiny roots that drink it in. Maybe consider planting smaller – there has been a vogue for large specimen plants, but they do need an awful lot of additional moisture in their first few years. Planting a small tree encourages the roots to set out on their own – it weans them early.

If you are planning on building a new property, sink some underground tanks made of reinforced concrete steel or plastic so that whatever drains off your property can be stored for use in your garden. Grey water from washing in the house is fine for all plants, particularly if you use ecological soaps and detergents, so don't be afraid to reuse the water that would otherwise get drained off for treatment.

Think about the lawn. We grow the best lawns in the world, but are they worth it? It takes an incredible amount of moisture to keep them lush and green. It's just possible that our gardening standards will have to drop a little as our care for the environment rises correspondingly.

Paul's plant of the month

Roscoea

Roscoea are fascinating plants and unlike any other herbaceous plants in terms of foliage and flowers. They are actually members of the ginger family, which is evidenced when chopping back the stems, as they often emit a faint ginger smell. The biggest issue with *Roscoea* is their reluctance to wake up! They don't usually appear above ground until May, by which time there's so much else happening you tend to forget about them. Their orchid-like flowers come in various shades of purple to white and stand at the top of the thick, fleshy stems that are wonderful foliage plants in their own right. Once the frosts arrive in autumn the foliage dies back down to the ground, and you won't catch a glimpse until next May.

Summer exotica

PAUL

The best example I know of this style of gardening in Ireland is Jimi Blake's Hunting Brook Gardens in Blessington, County Wicklow. As well as using tender exotics, Jimi includes bright bursts of colour with the neon pink and yellow dahlia 'Bright Eyes', orange cosmos, rich scarlet monarda, zingy orange geums and a sprinkling of red salvias to create a joyful tapestry of different textures, shapes and colours. He also uses tender exotics to great effect by planting table-height troughs on his veranda and cramming them with cacti and succulents – it's fun, different and, as it doesn't need much watering, low-maintenance as well.

Tender exotics planted among 'normal' perennials gives a tropical, jungly feel. Yes, these plants need to be moved indoors for winter, in most areas, but since we have the climate in summer, it's fun to mix up the usual with some striking species.

Aeoniums

Aeoniums are evergreen succulents that come from the Canary Islands and Madeira. They will only survive outdoors in very mild coastal areas in Ireland and the UK – for example, they flourish in great numbers in Tresco Abbey Gardens in the Scilly Isles. However, for most of us, they need to be brought indoors over winter. That's not just because they are susceptible to frost – sitting outdoors in puddles of rain will rot them.

The smaller ones look wonderful planted in pots, but for maximum drama, plant the larger ones among your borders. *Aeonium arboretum*, the tree houseleek, forms a shrub a couple of feet tall. The most striking and best-known variety is 'Zwartkop', which has large glossy purple to almost black leaves clustered in big rosettes.

They like to be planted in well-drained soil, so add some grit if necessary – they'd also be very happy in a gravel garden. They're quite easy to propagate from cuttings. Our top tip is to let the bottom of the cutting form a callous overnight before potting into gritty compost – this will reduce the chance of rot.

Opposite: Japanese anemones add late-summer drama.

Banana plants

The luscious leaves of the banana plant are superb, setting the scene for a tropical atmosphere as well as bringing height and freshness to exotic planting. No urban jungle is complete without them. With all bananas, a little shelter from strong winds is advisable, as the leaves can tear.

Musa basjoo
Musa basjoo is the hardiest of the bananas, but it should still be treated as a tender perennial, moved to a frost-free area over winter and planted out when the frosts have passed. They can be kept outside and wrapped in horticultural fleece in milder areas.

Musa sikkimensis
This plant has narrower leaves with tropical burgundy stripes and mottling on both leaf surfaces. The fruits on these bananas don't taste good, but they are worth growing for their architectural paddle-shaped leaves.

Ensete ventricosum 'Maurelii'
Also known as the Abyssinian banana, this has pleasing purple-tinged leaves.

Cannas

Cannas are another good option for mixing it up in the herbaceous border. Grown for their large dramatic leaves, cannas also produce tropically bright flowers late in the summer. 'Durban' is a stunning variety with red and yellow striped leaves; 'Wyoming' has deep crimson stems and orange flowers; and *Canna* × *ehemanii* has deep green leaves and red flower heads. Cannas are originally from tropical and subtropical regions of South America and therefore should be treated as tender perennials.

Opposite: *Ensete ventricosum* 'Maurelii'.

Ginger

Cautleya and *Hedychium* are both members of the ginger family and do really well in these islands. To guarantee they come back they are best treated like dahlias: lift them as soon as the foliage blackens and store them under a cover until spring. *Cautleya spicata* 'Bleddyn's Beacon' is a taller, vigorous variety with lovely red and yellow flowers. *Hedychium coccineum* 'Tara', with its large foliage and orange flowers, really makes a statement, while *H. gardnerianum* has the most fantastic large pale-yellow flowers, which, as an added bonus, are scented.

Below left: *Dahlia* 'Honka Black'.
Below right: Dahlias add a touch of the exotic to any garden.
Opposite, top: Lilium henyri.
Opposite, bottom left: A banana plant's dramatic leaves.
Opposite, bottom right, and over: *Hedychium coccineum* 'Tara'.

Ricinus (castor oil plant)

Finally, *Ricinus*, the castor oil plant, brings a touch of exotica to the garden with some dramatic foliage. The leaves are bold and tinged with purple. It's a fast-growing plant that's easy to grow from seed and is best treated as an annual.

Later summer colour

In our gardens, seasons can melt into each other – there's no definite start or finish time for summer outdoors. So it's good to encourage some late-summer planting of herbaceous perennials to cheer up the dwindling hours of daylight. Our soil takes a while to cool down; it's a bit like a hot water bottle – even after we start to feel the chill, it retains heat like a warming blanket, eager to embrace fresh new pots of plants direct from the garden centre. And there's a host of choices to brighten up your borders in late summer. Here are just a few of our favourites.

Dahlias

Ever since the gardener Christopher Lloyd introduced the dahlia 'Bishop of Llandaff' to his hot border in Great Dixter, this has been a must-have plant for discerning plant lovers. It gives so much deep red value at this time of the year, one not to be missed. 'Verrone's Obsidian', 'Sam Hopkins', 'Thomas A. Edison', 'Night Butterfly', 'Kelsey Sunshine', 'Happy Halloween', 'Franz Kafka', 'Honka Black' and 'Totally Tangerine' are just a few of our favourites. The selection available is both daunting and incredible, so there will be a dahlia out there to suit any garden.

Echinacea purpurea (purple coneflower)

This coneflower has startlingly beautiful vivid pink flowers and is quite a tall plant. Don't plant just one – splash out and create a drift of three or five. A year or two down the line, as with most herbaceous perennials, you can divide and replant, so your summer will seem never-ending.

Schizostylis coccinea (crimson flag lily)

Like gladioli, we have different opinions on this plant – it just doesn't do it for Diarmuid, but Paul loves it, and it's a useful plant for later in the year. With its delicate sword-like foliage and starry flowers, it's certainly cheerful.

Coreopsis

Now, these are beautiful. Cheerful yellow daisy-like flowers – they're a must.

Astrantias

Astrantias are fantastic. With their lace-like foliage and wonderful frothy papery flowers, they're best planted in drifts. As with many of these recommendations, they are lovely as cut flowers for the vase.

Penstemons

Penstemons should be in everybody's garden – they flower for so long and they are such a simple cottage garden delight. 'Sour Grapes', 'Garnet' and 'Electric Blue' are all varieties we grow and love.

Opposite: Late summer hedgerows in Kerry are electric with fuchsia and crocosmia.

Aster × frikartii 'Mönch'

This is a Michaelmas daisy with lavender-blue flowers that will see you through October as well – it is delightful. An equally good option, which grows a little more compactly, is *Symphyotrichum* 'Little Carlow', which, despite the name, has no obvious connection to County Carlow.

Verbena bonariensis

Verbena bonariensis has become enormously popular in recent years. It's tall, with delicate hazy purple flowers that pair beautifully with grasses for an unstructured, informal look. It's great value as it flowers throughout the summer and well into the autumn.

Leucanthemum × superbum (shasta daisy)

The shasta daisy provides masses of flowers as long as you keep deadheading them. Gorgeous stuffed into pots on a sunny patio.

Opposite: A late-summer border in Altamont Gardens.
Above: *Symphyotrichum* 'Little Carlow'.
Left: Crocosmia are great late-summer flowers.

Rooftop and balcony gardens

Rooftops provide little shelter, so they're colder and more exposed than gardens at street level and this is important to remember when choosing plants for such situations. Down below, at ground level or in courtyards in the city, the heat and shelter provided by buildings create microclimates where even slightly tender plants can survive.

But further up, whether on a balcony or on the rooftop, you need to choose plants that are tough enough to brave the elements, that won't be blown to bits by the wind or freeze in the chill. Summertime also brings challenges in these exposed areas – where there is no shelter from sunshine, plants will dry out very quickly. Many terraces or balconies are situated beneath another balcony, so you can't rely on rainfall to keep plants moist.

Types of plants

The plants that will do best in these elevated situations are those that also thrive by the sea or are drought-resistant. Their leaves are adapted to withstand the desiccating effects of salt-laden winds and to retain moisture. For example, the leaves of escallonia are slightly sticky, which repels salt, Elaeagnus has leathery leaves with a silvery underside, and hebes have double-thickness leaves.

Silvery-looking shrubs such as lavender, santolina, stachys, corokia and olearias have fine layers of hair that protect leaves from drying out. Dwarf pines, with their needle-like leaves, and grasses and sedges are also suitable, as are plants with tough leaves like phormiums and cordylines.

Opposite: Diarmuid plants tender house-plants in his pots on the veranda balcony.

Of course you'll also want colour – again, think resilient seaside plants like pinks, thrift, valerian, osteospermum and erigeron.

Types of containers

The type of container you use is also important. Small terracotta pots will dry out very quickly, but there are plenty of other options that are non-porous, such as metal, plastic, fibreglass and resin. Ensure they are suitable for outdoors and won't crack or deteriorate through exposure to ultraviolet light.

Metal

If you are using metal pots make sure that they are suitable for wet environments. Mild steel will rust unless it has been powder-coated, galvanised or painted with a water-resistant coating. With metal containers we often try to provide some insulation by introducing a coating of foam or polystyrene sheeting between the compost and the outer metal layer. Galvanised steel dustbins are an inexpensive option, once they have had some drainage holes drilled at the bottom, and galvanised buckets are a favourite of Paul's for his tulip displays.

Wooden

If you are using wooden containers they need to be treated with a preservative. Wherever you are siting them, allow for good airflow all around so they won't rot. Old wine or vegetable crates can double up as plant containers – line with hessian or moss to contain the compost.

Specimen choice and container choice are key. As with all container gardening, you're responsible for the plants' feeding and watering requirements as they are not able to obtain this for themselves from the earth. Simple irrigation systems are your best bet for plants surviving in these situations – it need not be a huge investment but it's definitely worth it to keep your potted garden looking its best.

Opposite, top left: On Diarmuid's terrace he grows an entire garden in pots.
Opposite, top right: Beans grow happily in a repurposed oil drum.
Opposite, bottom right: Agapanthus are wonderfully tough plants for growing in pots.
Opposite, bottom left: Pots can be used in nearly any situation.

September

September is all about resurrection and redemption. On this island anyway, nine times out of ten September is the most beautiful month of the year. Life is back to some normality after the summer and you're in extra time. September is also the month of dahlia fetishising, because it's the only flower you need to grow this month. Late September is also a time of grief for the summer that was.

Opposite: Bowie posing in the *Geranium palmatum*.

Grasses

As summer fades into autumn, ornamental grasses prove their worth. Contemporary gardening relies on them to provide interest once colour has faded. Not only do they tend to come into flower later, but they are also often valuable as winter interest as their sheaf-like flowers retain their silhouettes. And as the sun gets lower in the sky, some magical effects can be achieved as the almost horizontal rays of sunshine illuminate their beauty.

They are relatively low maintenance, though the annual cutting back can be quite a job if you have a large plantation of them. For minimum maintenance choose evergreen varieties such as *Carex morrowii* (Japanese sedge), which only need a trim every few years to encourage fresh clean growth. And be aware that some grasses can be quite invasive. *Stipa arundinacea*, for instance, self-seeds everywhere.

Grasses have great versatility, with varieties available for both sunny and shady positions, damp and dry conditions. Taller columnar types make good focal points or upright accents in a border, while the fountain-shape types look really well in pots.

Read on for our collection of favourite grasses.

Opposite: *Austroderia richardii* – South American pampas grass.

Hakonechloa

Hakonechloa is the Japanese forest grass. It has a beautiful dome shape we use dotted through mixed borders. The surprise every year is the amazing orange autumnal colour – really beautiful and a great candidate for a large pot.

Stipa tenuissima

Stipa tenuissima is known as ponytail grass or Mexican feathergrass and is a small, fluffy blonde number – it loves the sun and is wonderful for introducing a light feathery effect.

Pennisetums

Many grasses invite you to feel their texture. Best among these are the pennisetums, with their fluffy bottlebrush flowers. *P. alopecuroides* 'Little Bunny' has delicate pink flowers, while *P. alopecuroides* 'Hameln' has purple-tinged plumes. A good choice for the mixed border or in patio pots.

Miscanthus

Miscanthus is one of the later grasses to flower. Generally they are best in a large garden as they are quite bulky and tall, for example *M. sacchariflorus*, which has large bamboo-like stems. For the smaller garden *M. sinensis* 'Morning Light', with creamy margins, would be better. Good flower tresses can remain over winter – cut back to the ground in spring.

Stipa gigantea

This is the graceful giant of the grass world, achieving heights of over 2.5 metres. A huge fountain of golden oat-like flowers makes this a dramatic specimen plant in any garden. It's a grass that doesn't like disturbance, so don't try division on this one.

Pampas grass

Pampas grass isn't everyone's cup of tea, but *Cortaderia richardii* is a more refined version well worth seeking out – it has very elegant arching plumes.

Imperata cylindrica 'Rubra'

If you like the unusual, you'll appreciate *Imperata cylindrica* 'Rubra', the Japanese blood grass. Flat lime-green leaves that turn blood-red from the tip towards the base make a dramatic display. Grow in full sun or partial shade, but keep them moist for optimal appearance.

Opposite: *Miscanthus* grass in early autumn.

Begin a compost heap

DIARMUID

A few years ago I began to compost seriously. It's a kind of alchemy: turning spent leaves, flowers and other organic matter from the garden into nutritious compost to be used for planting or mulching. It's become an addictive process.

Through the gardening year growth of all parts of plants accelerates, often at extraordinary rates. Controlling this growth often means cutting, chopping and weeding. Rather than exporting your green waste to landfill, why not create a compost heap?

You can construct a simple wooden version using old wooden pallets or crates, you could simply let green growth decompose in black plastic bags, or you could just layer courses of organic material on a piece of ground. You could also recycle an old rubbish bin by drilling some holes around the side. The main advantage of closed containers is that heat naturally builds during the decomposing process and in a container this will be retained, speeding up the process. Containers also keep any odours in and are less likely to attract pests.

To start the composting process, place a layer of small branches, twigs and leaves on the bottom of your newly created structure. This will allow some air to circulate. Then build up your green waste, layer after layer, including vegetable peelings from the kitchen along with the flowers you've dead-headed. More light twigs and branches can be followed by a layer of garden topsoil. The trick is never to use too much of any single type of organic waste matter in any layer. Never use any cooked leftovers from the kitchen.

Above left: Diarmuid on his new compost bins.
Above right: Who said compost isn't beautiful?
Left: Three-bay compost bins made from corrugated sheeting.

Filler plants for cracks and crevices

Hard landscaping such as patios, terraces and pathways are the building blocks of any garden. However, any feature using concrete, gravel, brick or stone can look harsh without the softening addition of plants.

There's a useful group of plants that grow quite happily when squeezed into gaps between paving stones or into crevices in stone walls and they will soften straight lines as well as bringing colour, flowers and sometimes scent. They can bring an informal charm to uninteresting patios or can be a cheap way of disguising paving that needs repair. You can also lift an entire slab or piece of paving and plant up the space created, bringing interest to a monotonously grey area. And if these plants colonise the gaps, it means weeds have less of a chance to invade.

As with any planting, you need to consider the aspect – is it a shady or open sunny spot? And in the case of pathways, how much foot traffic do you anticipate? Some plants, such as thyme, are pretty happy with being trodden on and will release their delicious scent as you walk on them; others, such as chamomile, will only tolerate occasional footfall.

Here's our selection for different situations.

Erigeron karvinskianus (Mexican fleabane)

This is a great little daisy. The flowers range from white to deep pink and will keep coming right through to October. It's very happy in a sunny, dry location and good for wildlife gardens as bees and butterflies like it too.

Thyme

Thyme is a great choice for filling spaces where paving slabs have been laid leaving gaps of a few inches for planting in between them. This robust plant will enjoy the dry poor soil that inevitably accompanies paving work. The reward – cushions of pale purple flowers and a delicious scent underfoot.

Mentha requienii (Corsican mint)

Corsican mint will release a zesty peppermint fragrance and won't be downtrodden if you walk on it. It prefers a little moisture and it's good in partial shade. It's one of the smallest mints, with dainty leaves, and it bears tiny mauve flowers in summer.

Left: Paul in Diarmuid's garden.

Aubretia

Aubretia looks pretty tumbling from walls or sprawling across rockeries with its vibrant blue and purple flowers. As it performs well on poor soil, this is also a good choice for gravelled areas. Cut back after it has flowered in spring and you may get a second flowering in summer.

Above: *Erigeron karvinskianus* growing on a wall.

Leptinella squalida 'Platts Black'

This plant looks a bit like a miniature fern witth feathery dark leaves. It's well able to creep along cracks and crevices. It's also known as brass buttons for the little yellow flowers it produces in summer. Grow in sun or partial shade.

Soleirolia soleirolii (mind your own business)

Soleirolia soleirolii or mind your own business looks a bit like moss and enjoys similar conditions – damp and shady. Like moss, it's a weed when you don't want it, but it can create beautiful effects to give an aged effect to paving, statuary or around ponds. It's a creeping perennial and can disappear after frost but will resume services in spring. There's a lime-green variety, 'Aurea', which will bring some brightness to dark areas.

Ground cover

There's a way of planting in parts of your garden that can achieve a both attractive and practical solution to garden maintenance – it's called ground cover. This doesn't refer to a particular species of plants but the job that many plants can do if planted closely together as a group to form a continuous mat across the soil. Think of it as a green carpet.

The primary reason for using ground cover is to suppress weeds that would otherwise flourish in bare soil, so it's a low-maintenance and environmentally friendly way to banish weeds. Ground cover can also unify a planting scheme by providing a pleasing backdrop. It's a handy solution to tricky spaces like slopes that are hard to maintain and can be an alternative to lawns that are high maintenance.

We see this in nature – if you walk into a woodland at different times of the year and observe the planting, you can see that what happens in nature can also be replicated in your plot. The forest floor may be carpeted in wild garlic or beautiful bluebells – they are doing so well that nothing else can compete.

Depending on your site and situation, you can choose plants that will form a blanket over soil, which looks good for a lot of the year and leaves no room for other undesirable plants or weeds to invade.

So how do you create a magic carpet in your plot? First you need to remove any existing weeds, making sure that you start with a clean, uncluttered surface. Most plants will do better in enriched soil, so add in some organic matter such as compost or well-rotted manure. You'll also need some mulch such as a fine bark to cover any bare soil that is left after planting – this will suppress weeds until your ground-cover plants start to knit together and dominate.

Now select your species. You want plants that will spread but not so vigorously that they become a problem themselves. Ideally choose plants that are evergreen, low-maintenance, look good and flourish in your particular site and microclimate.

PAUL

In my garden Pachyphragma macrophyllum has happily self-seeded and is slowly carpeting a few tricky areas. Its brilliant white flowers shine in a dark corner of the garden at a time when very little else is looking good!

Opposite, top left: Anemone carpeting the ground in spring.
Opposite, top right: A carpet of *Cyclamen coum.*
Opposite, middle right: Geraniums make great ground cover.
Opposite, bottom right: Epimedium is an excellent ground-cover plant.
Opposite, bottom left: *Geranium palmatum* in Diarmuid's garden covers a wide area.
Opposite, middle left: *Pachyphragma macrophyllum.*

Epimediums

We use epimediums a good deal – once established they smother the possibility of any weeds and we love them for their heart-shaped foliage and delicate flowers in spring. Good for dry shade, where they will form soft bushy mounds.

Pachysandra terminalis 'Green Carpet'

This is an evergreen, low-rise 'shrubette'. Also known as Japanese spurge, it has handsome glossy green-toothed leaves and white flowers in summer. Useful for partially or fully shaded areas, it will form a mat of green, just as long as the soil doesn't dry out.

Heucheras

Heucheras are well-behaved ground-cover plants – they don't invade but gently increase their girth. The vast range of foliage colours gives you plenty of choice from deep purples through oranges to limey greens.

Geraniums

Hardy geraniums are one of the easiest perennials to grow and tolerate most soils. Some, for example *Geranium macrorrhizum*, are semi-evergreen, so will maintain coverage against weeds all year. Or try G. 'Ann Folkard' for summer ground cover – her chartreuse green foliage topped with hundreds of deep magenta flowers will scramble gently through your borders.

Bergenia cordifolia (elephant's ears)

An excellent ground cover for dry shady places – one of the most difficult types of soils to plant – it's known as elephant's ears for the shape of its foliage, and its thick green leaves are also tough, like an elephant's hide. It's evergreen, with leaves developing a bronzy tint in winter, very hardy and produces sturdy stems topped with clusters of small pink, ruby-red or white flowers, depending on the cultivar.

Vinca (periwinkle)

Periwinkle is a vigorous spreader that will save you hours of weeding, offering evergreen coverage 365 days a year with some lovely violet flowers in spring. It's adaptable to most soils, spreading over rocks, up banks and under trees. A word of warning, though – only plant it where you really want it to take over, so not in your herbaceous borders.

Pachyphragma macrophyllum

This is an underused plant that deserves wider use in our gardens. It's evergreen, flowers early in spring and will grow in dry shade or a sunnier position. It makes a good ground cover and is easily controlled. If you can't find plants, try to get your hands on some seeds.

October

October is simply the best. The rich russet tones mark the end of the gardening year. Gusty days in October will strip the best of the colour from the plants, and you'll be left with the bones of the garden. But the sunlight on an October day is magic. Unusually for a time that isn't defined by growth, October has huge energy. It calls you. It's a time for making plans, and the ground isn't soaked or frozen – yet. There's clarity in the air, and you can see the skeleton of your garden. Both the joys and mistakes of the last season have been wiped away and you get another chance at a fresh start. It's confession and absolution all in one.

Opposite: *Acer palmatum* 'Bloodgood'.
Right: Butter-yellow foliage of *Lindera obtusiloba*.

Seed saving

PAUL

The seeds of a few plants, such as hellebores and primroses, are best sown 'green', or fresh, from the seed pods. I like to collect them straight off the plants and immediately plant the seed. This means that they germinate instantly rather than drying out and going into dormancy. Other seeds that can be sown straight away are astrantia, foxgloves, angelica, aquilegia, meconopsis, primulas, orlaya and delphiniums. If in doubt about whether you can save and successfully grow the seed of a particular plant, just give it a go! You'll be amazed how easily some plants germinate and very soon you'll have hundreds of plants to give away or, better still, swap with a gardening friend.

As the summer draws to a close it's the perfect time to think about collecting seed from a few favourite plants.

Did you know that in the UK there is a bunker where scientists are trying to collect a sample of seed from every known plant in existence? The Millennium Seed Bank in Wakehurst Place in Sussex is a sort of back-up facility where seeds are stored in case some dreadful natural event happens in a region where the seed is native and the plants are lost for ever. It is a zoo for seeds, the largest off-site conservation programme in the world. The seed bank stores an incredible 2.4 billon seeds and this insurance policy for nature has already been used to help re-establish areas of Australian bush that were destroyed by wildfires.

Seed saving is a craft we've practised for thousands of years, mostly in agricultural settings, the grains being dried and stored for use through the year. You can harvest seed from one plant for generations; we've heard of a family who have saved seed from a runner bean every year since before the Second World War! At the end of the season, they simply left a few beans to mature, ripen and dry and then the following spring they could sow this seed, and so it went on for years. This is often how lost or forgotten crops come back into production.

Irish Seed Savers was founded to preserve old, often forgotten, varieties of fruit and vegetables. Some of these old varieties grow on, often in remote farms and in gardens around the country, tended for years by successive generations and the seed carefully saved every year. These old varieties can have better flavour than many modern varieties that have been bred for productivity over flavour. Scientists and breeders have become increasingly interested in these varieties in recent years as they also tend to have more natural disease resistance than overbred modern varieties. They are keen to breed this back into new crops, especially as we move away from relying so heavily on chemicals to control problems.

As gardeners it's fun to save our own seed. It saves money while also being extremely satisfying and a quick way to propagate a large number of plants.

A seedling is genetically different from its parent plant, just as humans are all genetically different. Clones, like Dolly the sheep, are exact replicas of their parents, so they are identical in every way (they have the same flowers, foliage, etc.). So, when you sow the seeds of a purple aquilegia, for example, it isn't guaranteed that the offspring will be purple, especially if it grows near another aquilegia with different colours. It may indeed germinate and eventually flower purple, but it is a gamble, a rather glorious gamble. Either way you'll get a good homegrown plant that will be well suited to your garden, especially if the parents already grow happily there.

Above: Aquilegias are prolific seed producers.

Some plants, like sweet peas, will come true to their parents and they're less of a gamble, so for that reason they are an excellent plant to save your own seed from, particularly if they're a variety or colour you love.

Most seeds are best saved in autumn, stored over winter and sown the following spring, when conditions are more favourable. Choose a dry day and simply place a paper bag over the seed head when you begin to see seed fall from it. If you take seed too early, it may not be ripe enough to germinate, so wait until the seed falls from the plant with the slightest touch. Once the paper bag is over the seed head, simply close it around the stem and cut the stem. Then turn the seed head upside down and shake it to allow the seed to fall into the bag. Sometimes it is worth leaving the seed in a cool dry room for a few days to allow it to fully dry and the seed pods to open.

You can then package the seed into paper envelopes, making sure to label carefully as you go! Paper envelopes are best as paper breathes, and if it gets wet it will dry out, unlike plastic bags, which can often trap moisture and encourage the seed to rot. Ideally, sow your seed next spring at the latest and don't store it for too long, although some seed can remain viable for decades and occasionally hundreds of years. Dock seeds can remain viable in the ground for seventy years!

Above: Cleaning of fleshy seeds.
Opposite, left: Vibrant pink flowers of *Nerine bowdenii*.
Opposite, right: Autumn crocus or *Colchicum*.
Over: *Sorbus aucuparia* (rowan) produces masses of berries.

Autumn-flowering bulbs

Bulbs don't just flower in the spring; early autumn brings a whole new flush of flowering bulbs to the garden. Some can really brighten up the often cooler, damper days of October.

Nerine bowdenii (Guernsey lily)

This late-flowering bulb will really brighten up a dull day with its vivid bright pink flowers. The lily-like flowers are all the more eye-catching as they are carried on bare stems (the leaves appear in spring but die down over summer). It comes from southern Africa, so it needs a really sunny, sheltered, warm position; the base of a south-facing brick wall would be ideal. It may take a year or two to bulk up, but once it feels at home it will flourish. It doesn't enjoy sitting in wet soil, so a well-drained position is best, and you might need to provide some protection if the weather gets very cold this winter.

Colchicum (naked ladies)

Called naked ladies because the stem and flower emerge in autumn bare of leaves, *Colchicum* are also known as autumn crocus because they look very similar to the familiar spring-flowering crocus. Plant in July or August for autumn flowering. The leaves then emerge in spring and die down in the summer. Our native *C. autumnale* (meadow saffron) grows wild in damp meadows, and in the garden they will prefer moisture-retentive soil. The showiest of the species is *C. speciosum* 'Album', which has beautiful pure white flowers. A word of caution, however – the plant is highly toxic if ingested and the bulbs have sometimes been mistaken for edible wild garlic, leading to accidental poisoning.

Arum italicum
(Italian lords-and-ladies)

If you've visited the woods recently you might have spotted this native herbaceous perennial. In the summer all you will see is a spike of bright orange berries sticking out of the ground. Be careful of these as they are poisonous. It waits until autumn for its handsome leaves to emerge, which, after the plant sends up a flower in spring, completely disappear for the rest of the year. There is a marbled-leaf variety called 'Marmoratum', which is very attractive, with arrow-shaped leaves with creamy-white veins, and excellent ground cover for this time of year. Plant in sun or partial shade in moist, well-drained soil.

Cyclamen hederifolium

Cyclamen grow well from seed, or plant now while in foliage and bloom. They like semi-shade, so they are great for colonising under trees, and the marbled green leaves will provide interest for most of the year. The result is masses of pale pink flowers nodding on naked stems, an amazing show of unexpected pastel colour when trees and shrubs are starting to turn orange and yellow in anticipation of winter.

Below: *Cyclamen hederifolium* – autumn cyclamen.

No dig

We have been influenced and inspired by a recent chat with the wonderful Charles Dowding, a gardening guru who since the 1980s has pioneered the practice of 'no dig' organic gardening. No dig is a philosophy and way of gardening that does what it says on the tin – it's about putting aside your spade and leaving the soil undisturbed as much as possible. This allows all soil life, including microbes and earthworms, to proliferate and protects the delicate matrix that is soil structure. Every time we rotavate or dig, we are breaking down that structure. So, before we rush out to dig over our plots, let's take some time to consider this hands-off method of gardening.

Charles became interested in growing his own veg when he became a vegetarian at university. He started an organic market garden and was always interested in the connection between the soil, plants and our own nutritional health. He eschewed the chemicals and fertilizers so predominant in gardening in the 1970s and 1980s, believing that if you get the biology of the soil right, your plants will be able to access the nutrients they require.

He observed that other market gardens were overrun with weeds such as chickweed and fat hen, and digging them up took up a lot of time. Moreover, he noted, bare soil cleared of weeds will soon be covered with weeds again. As he puts it, 'I think of soil as a living organism. When the soil is disturbed, weeds are part of the "recovery" process. Leave the soil alone and it becomes calmer.' And when we dig over soil, we also bring seeds to the surface that germinate in the light.

So, instead of digging, he buries weeds with a thick mulch of compost or layers of cardboard. This can be anything from 5 to 15 centimetres deep, enough to exclude light from weeds, which in turn suppresses their growth. In the case of really difficult and invasive weeds such as bindweed, which will grow through the cardboard, he advises keeping pulling the plant out – persistence

Paul's plant of the month

Lindera obtusiloba

Lindera are a lesser-known group of plants in the laurel family that have some great qualities as garden plants. *Lindera obtusiloba*, or the blunt-lobed spice bush, is a fantastic very small tree – or large shrub – that has masses of bright yellow flowers in early spring, when little else is out. They are deciduous and flower on bare stems. Their real moment to shine is this time of year, when the lobed foliage turns the most intense butter-yellow, catching everyone's attention and filling the garden with their richly coloured foliage.

will pay off. Mulches he uses include garden compost, spent hops, coffee grounds, mushroom compost and horse manure. As well as blanketing the weeds, this organic material creates a hive of activity in the soil, such as earthworms moving through the soil digesting organic matter and creating air pockets. By doing this, you not only leave the original soil structure intact but also enrich it. This helps with drainage in wet weather as well as water retention in dry periods.

How can you implement this no-dig regime in your garden? Charles advises starting off small. You can build a raised bed over your soil or lawn, fill it with compost and you are ready to plant. Small weed seedlings can be lightly hoed off in spring, but just skim the surface with a light touch. This is best done on a dry day when weeds will shrivel up. Other weeds can be pulled by hand as they emerge. The first year is the hardest, with a proliferation of slugs, but as things improve and the weeds disappear, your veg patch will actually become less work as you completely ditch that back-breaking digging.

Autumn colour

Many of the big trees that have magnificent autumn colour, such as oak and beech (unless as a hedge), are not suitable for the average garden. It's a great spectacle to see a liquidambar, tulip tree or gingko put on its annual performance, but if you have a small or average-sized plot, what species are suited to your garden?

DIARMUID

From October many of the leaves on the sixty-plus trees in my smallish garden begin to change colour from green to the most exciting tones of yellows, reds and browns – colours so vibrant that when glimpsed in sunlight they become as joyous as the brightest summer blossoms.

Average-sized plot

Japanese maples
Japanese maples are the top choice as they are slow growing and will do well in a container if necessary. There are wonderful varieties that have different foliage colour and dissected leaf shapes. The key thing to remember with these exotic beauties is shelter – they won't do well being blown to bits and they don't like to bake in the sunshine either, so partial shade is best.

Prunus sargentii (Sargent's cherry)
Sargent's cherry puts on a fantastic display of flaming leaves in the autumn. It's the best cherry for multi-season interest – fabulous pink blossoms in spring, followed by bronze juvenile foliage that turns green in summer and ends up bright orange and red in autumn. However, it can eventually grow quite large – up to 9 metres. So for the smaller garden consider *Prunus* 'Amanogawa', which has a slender shape and good autumn colour, or *P. incisa* 'Kojo-no-mai', which is a shrub cherry that can be grown in a pot and has vivid pigments this time of year.

Parrotia persica (ironwood tree)
The ironwood tree is unsurpassed for the blushing reds, pinks, plums and yellow tones it takes on in autumn, but its wide, spreading shape is a bit greedy for space. We both grow 'Vanessa', which has a narrow upright habit, making it a less obtrusive guest in the garden, but it still has the wow factor.

Some other ideas
Other choices for autumn colour are *Cercidyphyllum*, whose dainty leaves turn pink and delightfully smell of burnt toffee; *Viburnum farreri*, which is grown for its fabulous scented winter flowers, but the red leaves in autumn are a bonus; and the rowans (*Sorbus*), the unsung heroes of the suburban landscape with their amazing berries and seasonal colour changes.

Smaller plots

How can we fully achieve the magnificence that autumn can bring in a really small garden, using trees and shrubs that don't require the room that enormous estates allow? Here's our choice for smaller plots.

Acer japonicum 'Aconitifolium'
The full moon maple is one of the best Japanese maples for autumn colour, its ferny palmate leaves turning vivid red and orange. For best results grow in dappled or partial shade with protection from cold winds. Beautiful as a specimen tree in a patio or courtyard situation.

Liquidambar
Liquidambar or sweet gum trees produce some of the best autumn colours, a wonderful mix of plum, red and orange maple-like leaves. However, as they grow to over 22 metres in maturity, they're usually unsuitable for small to average plots. 'Slender Silhouette' is a lovely upright cultivar which, while it grows tall, remains slimline. Sweet gums prefer dampish, neutral to acidic soil.

Acer griseum (paper bark maple)
How could one ever tire of the wonderful coppery peeling bark of this maple? And there's more reason to love it in autumn when its leaves turn to a burning red and orange. A delightful specimen for any garden.

Cotinus 'Royal Purple'
Grow the smoke bush for its beautiful purple foliage that turns scarlet in autumn. The 'smoke' part of its name derives from the frothy plumes of delicate flowers in summer that look like a haze of smoke around the plant. It likes full sun in a moist but well-drained soil.

Opposite, top left: Japanese maples turn vibrant shades in autumn.
Opposite, top right: A spindle bush turning colour on a damp autumnal morning.
Opposite, bottom right: Autumn colours of *Crataegus persimilis* 'Prunifolia'.
Opposite, bottom left: *Acer* 'Bloodgood' in autumn light.

Cornus kousa 'Miss Satomi'
This is a good choice if you have room for a small tree or large shrub to spread laterally but you just don't want it to grow tall. The branches are outstretched, and the leaves turn purple and deep red in autumn.

Rhus typhina (staghorn sumach)
Staghorn sumach turns a vibrant shade of orange in autumn, and it's one of the most reliable small trees. If you want something a little bit different, go for 'Dissecta', which has finely dissected leaves, giving a more refined appearance. You will need to remove suckers as they appear to keep the plant contained.

Euonymus alatus
Spindle trees, or the burning bush, are unrivalled when it comes to fiery autumn colour. This, combined with their beautiful purple fruit, which splits open to reveal orange fruit, and their interesting textured bark, make them an outstanding small tree.

Sorbus 'Joseph Rock'
Sorbus, rowan or mountain ash is a great all-rounder for the small garden. Lots of creamy flowers in spring are followed by wonderful yellow berries in late summer, and in autumn the elegant pinnate foliage turns a deep crimson.

Crataegus persimilis 'Prunifolia'
Plum-leaved hawthorn is a great tree with many merits that's perfect for a small space. It has beautiful white flowers in spring, but it's the autumn display that this tree should be grown for. The foliage turns over a number of weeks, and when it eventually falls off the red berries will remain for a few weeks until the birds have their fill.

November

November is wet. The beautiful crisp leaves of October become soggy piles of mush and the garden retreats for its winter sleep. There is decay all around as the first frosts really bite and all of the lushness of summer is levelled to the ground. There's still lots to do, but we prefer to leave the garden as a habitat for wildlife as long as possible until spring.

Opposite: Winter foliage on *Quercus dentata* 'Carl Ferris Miller'.
Above left: A view of the veranda in November.
Left: Willow stems bring colour to the November garden.

Bulb lasagne

It's time to choose and plant your spring bulbs. Taking inspiration from the Italian culinary classic, lasagne, where pasta is layered with other ingredients, we're going to layer bulbs in pots to enable us to grow great combinations of bulbs in the same pot or to have a succession of bulbs that commence flowering in February and continue through to May. Add a few plants on top and you'll have six months of joy.

Container

Let's start with the container. The bigger the pot the better. If it's terracotta, it needs to be frostproof – there's nothing more disheartening than finding your creation in bits on a frosty morning. Drainage is always important with bulbs – soggy soil can cause them to rot. Adding some gravel or even bits of broken old pots to the bottom of the container will help. Compost needs to be free-draining but capable of holding moisture. You won't need to add feed as the new bulbs will have all they need to grow.

Ingredients

Next, the ingredients – a selection of bulbs that will flower at different times. When shopping, inspect bulbs before purchase. You wouldn't buy an onion bulb that was withered or diseased, and the same goes for your garden bulbs – they should be firm and healthy-looking. You could go for snowdrops and winter aconites for February, daffodils and fritillaria for March, grape hyacinths and early tulips for April and alliums and late tulips for May. The reality is that any bulbs you find in autumn can be planted in your lasagne pots.

Method

Use the largest and latest-flowering bulbs – for example, alliums and tulips – as the bottom layer. Don't pack them in too tightly – give them an inch or two to themselves. Now cover with a layer of compost and plant the next layer of bulbs, which will flower before the previous layer –

Opposite: Tulips in a lasagne pot show the layered effect.

for example, daffodils. You might stop at two layers; in which case, cover with a good helping of compost. Or you can go for a third layer of smaller, even earlier-flowering bulbs such as dwarf daffodil and *Iris reticulata*. Don't worry about planting bulbs straight on top of each other – they will always find a route through, even if they have to bend their stems around other bulbs. Bulbs planted the wrong way round will usually find their way to the light as well.

Some cyclamen, gaultheria, viola, pansies or primroses will help give your lasagne pot a splash of instant colour and the bulbs will easily find their way through these roots too. Now just water in and leave to chill for winter.

If you make them work hard, you can get at least six months of pleasure from pots planted this month.

Recipe combinations

Here are a few recipe combinations you could try – or have fun experimenting with different ideas yourself: it really is a case of anything goes.

Tulip delight

Try an early tulip such as the fragrant orange 'Princess Irene' and top with a sprinkling of purple crocus for a zingy combination.

Blue and white combination

Plant tulip 'White Parrot' at the bottom for a frilly white display in May, combined with blue hyacinth in the middle with a mix of muscari or scilla on top.

Pink and purple confection

Place *Allium* 'Purple Sensation' at the bottom, sandwich tulip 'Queen of the Night' in the middle and add a sprinkling of some *Anemone blanda* 'Pink Star' on top.

Daffodil surprise

Dwarf narcissus 'Tête-à-Tête' are great for pots and will usually be your top layer. But buried beneath can be some fritillaria bulbs, which are pretty big and will be a great follow-on surprise in early summer.

Left: This lasagne combination is at its peak.
Opposite, top left: Placing tulip bulbs so that they don't touch.
Opposite, top right: Crocus, daffodils and violas in a lasagne pot.
Opposite, bottom right: You should see the first signs of life early in the new year.
Opposite, bottom left: Daffodils work really well as the lower layers in lasagne pots.

Winter protection

The delight of gardening on these islands is that we have a temperate climate – a lack of extremes of hot and cold, wet and dry. For that reason we have been at the forefront of gardening and have gathered plants from all corners of the world to adorn our gardens, both public and private. We can grow a vast variety of plants from the Americas, Asia, Australia and Africa. In fact, if we didn't, our gardens would look very bare indeed. Think about it. Roses come from Asia, lavender from the Mediterranean, potatoes from South America, lupins from North America, wisteria from China and Japan, hydrangea from Asia and, of course, bamboo from many continents except Europe. The number of native ornamental plants in any garden is often relatively small. This brief list forms the backbone of many of our planting styles. And generally, the plants we use are pretty hardy. That means that, in most years, the winter won't do them in.

But we like to push things further and create a real sense of the exotic, so since we began as gardeners we have sought to fascinate ourselves and others with plants that are terribly exotic. Many of us grow begonias, dahlias and all kinds of colourful flowers. After recent terrible winters we have learned that some will need winter protection if they are to survive and thrive.

Why are freezing temperatures so damaging to plants? Well, when water freezes it expands, and when it does this in a plant cell, it breaks down the cell walls. If enough cells collapse, the plant withers and blackens. In addition, when the ground becomes frozen it can be difficult for even hardy plants to obtain moisture through their roots. As a result lots of plants actually die from drought in prolonged periods of extreme cold.

The simplest method of preventing winter damage is to bring your plants indoors into a conservatory or unheated greenhouse. Even an open veranda or somewhere close to the house's eaves will provide some protection. Some tender plants become dormant in the winter and can be lifted for overwintering – for example, cannas, dahlias, gladioli and begonias. You can also take cuttings of tender plants to ensure new stock for next spring. Pelargoniums or pot geraniums are easy to take cuttings from as a winter insurance policy. Of course, it's not just the plants that can be tender – pots can crack over winter too, so if you have a pot that's precious to you, bring it in. Keeping pots raised off the ground will also help as that gives them a chance to dry out between the showers.

If you can't bring plants indoors and need to protect them in situ, there are a variety of ways you can do so. Mulching around the base will help any plant, tender or not, survive the winter. This can be with straw, mulch, dead leaves or compost. You can also cover with horticultural fleece or polythene. Individual smaller species can be protected with cloches and larger species can be wrapped in hessian or even bubble wrap. Tree ferns will benefit from not only their trunks being covered, but also their crowns, where new growth emerges. Other at-risk plants include bananas, bay trees, cordylines, palms, echiums, pittosporum and *Acacia dealbata*. You can use dry leaves to protect dahlia tubers; fill a bell cloche with the leaves and place it over where the dahlias are growing once the frost has blackened all the foliage.

Snowfall is sometimes not as damaging as frost and can even insulate a plant against extreme temperatures. However, its weight can snap branches and splay hedges, so, if possible, remove excess snow from branches and the tops of shrubs. In areas of Japan that are hit every year by heavy snowfall, they create maypole-like structures made of a central stem of thick bamboo and strands of bamboo rope that are tied around the limbs of revered pines to take the weight of snow-laden branches. While you wouldn't do something as elaborate here, you could consider tying in pencil-shaped conifers so that they won't lose their shape.

Bare-root planting and native hedging

Before the advent of plastic pots, plants were often grown in rows in fields and the best time to buy and plant them was the dormant season – that is between November and the end of March, which is when plants in effect go to sleep for winter. Traditional bare-root planting has many advantages. The plants you'll buy like this in winter are easy to transport because of the lack of soil, and that often means that the plants will be considerably cheaper as they are easier to manage for the growers and retailers.

The lower transport costs and lack of plastic make this a more environmentally friendly approach as well. The plants will establish more quickly to their new environment and as they are lighter, they are easier to handle. It's also an ideal winter project – activity in the garden has slowed down, you have a bit more time and you don't have the worry of new plantings dying due to dehydration as you do in the summer.

What you will buy is plants with soil washed off the roots. It may seem strange, but if the plant's root system is kept nicely moist by being wrapped in material such as damp hessian, it will be perfectly viable. If you have large planting projects – lots of trees or a hedge, for example – it can cut your costs substantially, and it's a cheap way to buy rose and fruit bushes also.

Preparation is key for this type of planting. Your bare-root stock will not wait around (the roots can dry out), so prepare your planting pits before the plants arrive. If you can't plant immediately, you can heel them in – this means making a slit in the soil with your spade and popping the plant in until you're ready to plant. It's also recommended to soak the roots for 30 minutes prior to planting.

Choose a good day for planting. Avoid planting when ground is waterlogged as there is no oxygen available to the plant in these conditions and you will also be damaging soil by treading on it.

Heavy frosts can create problems too, making the ground hard to break with a spade and inhibiting roots. Heavy frosts can also lift new plants slightly out of the ground, exposing roots to the cold air, which isn't ideal. However, after a light frost can be a good time to plant as the earth will be crumbly and friable.

Break up the sides of the planting hole as well as the bottom to encourage roots to reach out. A small mound at the base of the hole will encourage water to drain away. Add in some slow-release fertilizer and compost. Current thinking favours putting in some mycorrhizal fungi, which encourages a mutually beneficial relationship between roots and soil. If you need to stake the plants, put the stake in now – plunging it in afterwards can damage roots. Plant at the same level the plant was planted at previously – just above the flare of the roots – you can usually make out a tide line of soil on the stem. Roses are the exception – plant these with the graft union about 7–8 centimetres below the soil – this is the swollen knobbly bit between the root system and the base of the stem. Backfill and tread in the soil to avoid leaving air pockets. Finally, water your new plant.

A native hedgerow supports a wide range of wildlife, from bees, butterflies and birds to badgers and bats. The flowers provide pollen, the branches nesting opportunities and the berries valuable winter food. Bats even use these hedges as a kind of satellite navigation system to guide them on their flight paths. Together, as these hedgerows criss-cross the country through farms and gardens, they form wildlife corridors, which are essential for a healthy ecology.

For the gardener, native hedges are reliable performers in tricky conditions. They are made up of native plants that have adapted to our climate and soil, so even when the earth is poor or damp or when the climate gets extreme, they're not going to faint and wilt. So whether you want a hedge or just have room for one plant, read on for our top choice of native hedgerow species.

Over: Autumn turns the countryside foliage near Diarmuid's garden golden.

Native hedgerow species

Guelder rose

The guelder rose isn't actually a rose, it's our native viburnum. It's one of the most ornamental of the hedgerow plants. Fresh green sycamore-like leaves turn red in autumn and its pretty lacecap white flowers are followed by glassy red berries that blackbirds, bullfinches and thrushes love.

Rosa canina (dog rose)

Rosa canina is a very prickly and fast-growing rose that flowers in May and June. The autumn hips that follow are extremely high in vitamin C and provide food for waxwings, tits, thrushes and finches.

Hawthorn

Hawthorn is the classic hedgerow plant and it's found in the majority of farmland hedges. It's dense, thorny and fast-growing, making it ideal as a barrier to livestock. It supports hundreds of insects and its flowers, berries and foliage create an interesting tapestry.

Buckthorn

Alder buckthorn (*Frangula alnus*) is a good choice for damper sites. It is one of the main food sources of the brimstone butterfly, whose caterpillars eat the leaves. Birds like to nest in the dense network of branches. Its wood is a source of charcoal, once used in gunpowder.

Blackthorn

Blackthorn produces white blossoms very early in the year, which is a boon for bees. Butterflies lay their eggs and in turn birds feast on the caterpillars. Then it's our turn in winter when we can pick the berries, known as sloes, and use them to make wine or gin.

Hazel

The hazel tree creates shelter for nesting birds and the nuts in autumn provide valuable hibernation food for squirrels. And it looks lovely draped in yellow catkins in February.

Holly

Holly provides dense cover for birds and, of course, those wonderful berries in winter. For the gardener, its handsome glossy evergreen leaves deliver structure and colour in the depths of winter.

Elder

Elder, or *Sambucus nigra*, produces creamy-white flat heads of flowers in summer followed by black berries, which are rich in vitamin C, though they should be cooked before eating. They provide good foraging for wildlife and humans – the flowers can be made into wine or cordial or even dipped in batter and fried as fritters. With its five-leaflet foliage, this plant will add layers of interest and texture to a hedge.

Opposite: Blossom on our native hawthorn.

Water features

Dynamic, beautiful, exciting, versatile and reflective, water has been a central feature in gardens throughout time. Once it was the preserve of the wealthy, who built aqueducts and canals to transport water many miles from river plains to arid deserts or to high Italian terraces. In the Alhambra gardens in Granada, Spain, the Moors built pools that reflected the grandeur of the buildings and mirrored the sky above. Fountains cooled the air by a few degrees in enclosed courtyards and provided restful babbling sounds.

Water was an essential component of Islamic gardens, where rills or canals represented ancient rivers from the east. An Islamic garden was an earthly representation of paradise (if you lived a virtuous life your afterlife was spent in a garden), but in paradise there would be four rivers – of milk, honey, wine and water.

At the Villa d'Este in Italy, water cascades through fountains and grottoes, a musical organ is played by the power of water, and stone galleons shoot water through their cannons, recreating historic sea battles of old. At the Palace of Versailles, fountains dance to classical music, and as the Sun King strode through his earthly paradise, a footman ran in front to turn on the next fountain while another ran behind to turn off the previous display. Water pressure wasn't what it is today!

All that is on a very grand scale, but water can perform many roles in your own garden, regardless of your plot size. Features such as wall and bubble fountains are useful for small gardens, patios and courtyards and offer sound, movement and dramatic focal points.

The first consideration with water is to make it safe for children, pets and wildlife. Ponds are not suitable for children as they can drown in even a few inches of water. It may not be your own child who is in danger – young friends or cousins can be enchanted by the notion of water and may disappear outdoors unsupervised to explore. So take precautions. If you have an existing pond, you can

Opposite: A wildlife pond can be hugely beneficial, even in a small garden.

cover it with a sturdy metal grille. You should also avoid slippery surfaces close to water to safeguard people of all ages.

But there are easier and cheaper alternatives to ponds and pools. A pot or barrel can be transformed into a mini-pond – make sure it has no drainage holes, and if using a terracotta pot, paint the inside with a waterproofing yacht varnish. Sit plants in their pots on bricks so their leaves just float on the surface. Keep it ultra simple and plant the pygmy water lily, *Nymphaea* 'Tetragona', one of the smallest water lilies, which has white fragrant flowers.

You don't need a great gushing fountain – the smallest trickle of water can be very relaxing. Simple pump and water reservoir kits allow you to recycle water, so it's not necessary to plumb water in, but you will need an electrician to safely connect up the pump – water and electricity is a dangerous combination when not properly installed. Water trickling through a jet over polished cobbles or pieces of slate can be extremely effective.

Reclamation yards can be great sources of unusual and good-quality fountains. And if space is really tight, considering installing a small water feature on a garden wall. This traditionally takes the form of a decorative plaque such as a wall-mounted lion's head spouting water into a receptacle, but contemporary effects can be achieved by water sheeting down a piece of glass or steel.

For oriental simplicity and serenity, the *shishi-odoshi* is a type of water feature found in Japanese gardens. It consists of a hollowed-out bamboo tube through which water trickles, causing the tube to tilt downwards, making a gentle knocking sound as it touches the bowl, and as it releases the water the tube then swings upwards again. Traditionally used to scare deer from grazing plants, there's something deeply hypnotic and restful about watching one of these in action.

Opposite: Japanese water iris, *Iris ensata*, line this formal canal in Bellefield gardens.

Paul's dream garden

Close your eyes and plant a garden. What does it contain? Where is it? What can you see? My answer is simple enough, although a visitor to my dream should bring a machete! And they should expect the unexpected.

My dream Eden is packed with plants. It's a paradise full of trees, shrubs, climbers, perennials, all growing in their place, full of colour, foliage and life. I'm a collector and hoarder of plants and my garden is filled with my favourites – snowdrops, daffodils, phlox, hydrangea and nerines.

There are birch woods and an oak forest, where the stars are the daimyo oak, *Quercus dentata* 'Carl Ferris Miller' and the northern red oak *Quercus rubra*, all thriving in the wonderful springy soil. But this Eden isn't just a forest – it has openings, prairies and deserts. I've planted acres of meadows flowering from spring through autumn, with finely cut pathways through them.

My paradise is filled with every plant imaginable, each considered and understood. Space isn't an issue, as this dream garden is larger than Dublin's Phoenix Park. The only problem is knowing where to stop with the planting! I'd want it all: the driest, most arid soil on a south-facing slope of the garden, with damp peatland at the other side, and you'd have to cross the tundra in between. Every habitat means endless possibilities to explore plant combinations and to figure out what plants will cope where and how to grow the most eclectic range.

At the heart of my garden is where I live – a corrugated tin structure smothered in climbers and vines. Beside the door are huge trunks of *Betula albinosis* 'Fascination', its smooth peeling bark almost blocking the way. Climbing hydrangeas, ivies and grape vines cover the structure, almost obliterating the light. I have the right plant for every place, the correct soil and the best aspect for everything. Gardening is about the plants, growing them, tending to them and seeing them thrive. I've created a garden that's miles from anywhere – I can get lost in it for days and spend endless summer evenings pottering until sunset.

My garden also has a Crystal Palace filled with oddities, rarities and tender plants. This other jungle is straight from an Indiana Jones adventure, warm, humid and overgrown as if abandoned for years, yet tended with the gentlest touch. A jungle, but a wonderful jungle.

Gardening here isn't about the end result. This creation will never be finished. Like all gardens, it's all about the process and the trials and tribulations by which we learn. My pleasure is in the dream and the beauty that exists in the act of gardening itself. When all's said and done, though, I'm happy here just as I am – pottering in whatever garden I'm allowed.

December

December is camp. Go into a garden centre in December and you'll be surrounded by plastic tack and fairy lights, which is basically what Diarmuid's garden is. We take the lead from holly berries and Coca-Cola's marketing department and feel that this is the way to go. December is enforced cheeriness, the season of purchase, the season of visitors, which means brightening up your spaces. Don't believe the hype – anything you do now will not survive in the long term. Azaleas will be short-lived and only bloom for a few weeks if you're lucky. Cyclamen will get eaten and frosted. December is lost dreams, lost causes and lost plants.

Opposite: Winter light in Paul's polytunnel.

Berries

Winter berries are an extraordinary gift that delight both us and many other creatures that rely on them for food. Berries ensure the survival of some species through the seeds they contain, which may go on to be germinated and become new young plants; they also provide food and energy for hungry garden birds. And, of course, berries can be brought indoors for decoration in the festive season and act as an indoor reminder of the wonders of the natural world outside.

Pyracantha

Among our favourite is pyracantha, if only for sheer reliability – heavy crops of bright orange, red or yellow berries. These make great displays when the plant is trained against a wall and kept well pruned.

Guelder rose

The guelder rose, *Viburnum opulus*, is a wonderful deciduous shrub with intricately cut grapevine-like leaves, bearing large pure white clusters of pom-pom flowers. The fruits are bright glassy red, a bit like bunches of shiny red marbles. The foliage colour in autumn is an added bonus as the yellowing leaves become a gorgeous red. The compact cultivar 'Compactum' is appropriate for any size garden and definitely worth looking out for.

Holly

Holly and its vivid red berries are synonymous with Christmas. In Christian symbolism the prickly leaves represent the crown of thorns, the berries the blood of Jesus.

Snowberry

The snowberry, *Symphoricarpos albus*, was widely planted in Victorian and Edwardian times in shrubberies and as game cover but is no longer popular, possibly due to its vigorous suckering and spreading habit. However, the plump white fruit is a gift to the birds at the moment and looks pretty in the hedgerows.

Sorbus hupehensis 'Pink Pagoda'

This mountain ash drips bunches of pink berries that fade to white in winter. It makes a wonderful specimen for a small back garden as it is petite but graceful in silhouette and has great autumn foliage as well. 'Pink Charm' is another good variety that has shocking pink berries.

Cotoneaster 'Rothschildianus'

For another unusual coloured berry, this cotoneaster has delicate light yellow fruits and, since it's an evergreen, is useful for year-round foliage.

Opposite: Skimmia are a favourite in December.

Callicarpa bodinieri var. geraldii 'Profusion'

For highly unusual coloured berries, this wins the prize. It will go unnoticed as a shrub for most of the year but come autumn it produces berries of a stunning lilac-purple hue. Best planted in groups for good cropping, it is aptly otherwise known as beautyberry.

Gaultheria mucronata

Also producing berries in the pink to purple colour range is *Gaultheria mucronata*. Related to the heather family, it needs lime-free soil to flourish and will look wonderful planted among its relations such as winter-flowering heathers.

Sea buckthorn

Seaside-dwellers will be familiar with the sea buckthorn, the hard-to-pronounce *Hippophae rhamnoides*. This is a great windbreak plant for coastal locations – it is thorny with narrow silvery leaves and glowing orange berries. The silver and orange make a striking combination.

Viburnum davidii

Viburnum davidii is so widely planted that we sometimes forget to appreciate its beauty. It has deeply veined evergreen leaves, and where several shrubs are planted together, they will produce vivid blue berries in winter.

Rosa rugosa

The hips of *Rosa rugosa* are a great injection of colour in the garden as the evenings begin to shorten – bright orange and red against the lime-green leaves of this rampant rose.

Heavenly bamboo

Nandina domestica, also known as heavenly bamboo, isn't a bamboo at all but has a similar growing habit. This shrub is a great all-rounder. It is evergreen in the sense that it doesn't lose its leaves, but its foliage turns reddish purple in spring and autumn. Panicles of small white flowers will produce red berries for the winter.

Propagation of berries

If you want to propagate from berries, you need to pick them when they are completely ripe – they should be soft when you squeeze them. Collect them and mash them through a sieve – a household one is fine – so that the pulp goes through and you are left with the seed in the sieve. Sow in gritty compost, covering the seeds lightly, and leave outside to germinate. Some may need more than one cold season to get going, so be patient!

Opposite: Crab apples are covered in jewels at this time of year.

Forcing bulbs

DIARMUID

It's a good idea to stagger hyacinth planting every two weeks so there are waves of fragrance to look forward to in the festive season. You can also plant them in special hyacinth vases – little bottles with a narrow neck for the bulb to rest in. Simply keep the water topped up to below – but not touching – the bulb and keep in a cool dark place.

Even in the middle of winter you can bring spring to your house, with a bit of forward planning. This is a practice known as 'forcing' bulbs to flower ahead of their time. By planting bulbs in late September and into October, you can have wonderful scented and colourful flowering displays indoors by Christmas.

Order some hyacinth bulbs – look for 'prepared' ones, as these have already been subjected to a cold spell to trick them that they are halfway through winter. If you are choosing different varieties, don't mix them up as they can flower at different times. The packaging will give you approximate times for flowering, so keep this info handy.

You'll also need some bulb fibre or multipurpose compost. Bulb fibre contains some charcoal, which keeps the compost sweet by absorbing gases, and this is particularly useful if you are using pots with no drainage holes.

When planting, wear gloves to protect your hands as hyacinth bulbs can cause skin irritation. Fill your pot with compost/bulb fibre, leaving a couple of inches for the bulbs. Place these on top, close but not touching, their noses pointing to the sky. Now fill in gaps with more compost – you want the tips of the bulbs to be visible at the top, not buried. Now water in so it's all moist – if you overdo the watering, just gently tip the pot to one side to drain off the excess. Place the pot in a cool (around 9°C) dark place – a shed or garage is ideal – and place a black polythene sack on top to exclude any light.

Depending on the variety, leave in situ for around six to eight weeks. Check them periodically and don't let them dry out. When about two inches of yellow growth is showing, bring the pots into the light – somewhere not too bright or too hot. Be patient – if you whip them out of the garage too early, you'll get lots of leaves but not much flower. Over the next three weeks they will green up and flower and be ready as gifts or to be brought into the warmth of the house.

'Amethyst' and 'Ostara' are great varieties for beautiful violet flowers, 'Delft' is the classic blue and 'Kronos' a very deep blue; 'Pink Pearl' and 'White Pearl' are good too. And they all smell fantastic.

Amaryllis can be tricked into flowering at Christmas by planting and watering them at the correct time for an even more dramatic display.

Left: Amaryllis are large dramatic flowering bulbs.
Over: Diarmuid's veranda comes to life in winter with these colorful Adirondack-style chairs.

Poinsettias

From giant succulents right the way through to the tiniest rock plants, euphorbias are a diverse and successful plant family. In the garden we're very familiar with varieties such as *Euphorbia characias* subsp. *wulfenii*, a handsome architectural plant with bold cylindrical heads of lime-green flowers that sit proudly on silvery-green leaves. It was greatly admired by Edwardian plantswoman Gertrude Jekyll and is found widely in herbaceous borders today. Another beauty in the family is *E. mellifera*, the honey spurge, which forms a beautifully rounded shrub with elegant foliage and honey-scented flowers in spring.

But perhaps the most successful of this tribe is *E. pulcherrima*, otherwise known to Christmas shoppers as poinsettia. Grown by the million for the festive season, they fill shelves and displays at DIY shops, supermarkets and garden centres and are purchased for indoor Christmas decorations and by last-minute shoppers as gifts.

Native to Mexico, this shrub was first discovered by the American ambassador to Mexico, Joseph Poinsett, a keen amateur botanist. He brought it back to the United States with him in 1828 and the rest is history. The cheerful red foliage has come to epitomise Christmas on both sides of the Atlantic. Legend has it that a poor young Mexican girl had no gifts to bring to the altar at Christmas so she gave what she could – some plants from the roadside, which then miraculously sprouted red blooms. The red blooms are actually leaves, called bracts, which are brightly coloured to attract pollinators.

Breeders continue to work on new variations all the time and today poinsettias are also available in cream and pink versions. There are very particular light and dark requirements to produce its brightly coloured bracts, which growers now have down to a fine art. You need a certain amount of dedication to do this at home and that's why many people will discard the poinsettia after the festive season. The tricky bit is trying to get the foliage to

Opposite: A greenhouse full of poinsettia ready for sale.

colour up in time for Christmas. The plant needs to be in complete darkness for 14 hours a day for at least eight weeks for the leaves to turn red. Start around next October to aim for red leaves for Christmas. Use black polythene or somewhere that's completely dark for 14 hours and then during the day bring the plant back out to good daylight conditions.

It's always good to know a plant's origins if you are keen to know how to look after them. Poinsettia comes from a dry, sunny country and will display signs of homesickness, such as shedding its leaves, if you don't make it feel at home. Therefore, to keep it happy, don't expose it to any cold draughts. This includes the journey home from the garden centre or when bringing it as a gift.

Try to position it somewhere in the house that isn't susceptible to sudden draughts – halls and porches aren't the most suitable spots. As a tropical plant it will enjoy good light, but keep it away from direct sunlight. While it likes it warm, don't put it in front of direct heat such as radiators or fires. There's no need to sit your poinsettia in a tray of water – just water carefully when the soil is dry to the touch. As with most indoor plants, the most common cause of plant failure is under- or over-watering, so try to strike a balance. With a little care, you can enjoy the festive foliage for many months to come.

Opposite: Late autumn in Wicklow.

Evergreen perennials

We don't normally associate perennial plants with the off-season, late autumn through winter. Perennials are a group of plants that come back from year to year but don't form woody stems. As the mainstay of our traditional flower borders, they are grown for their beautiful blossoms and interesting foliage. But we don't have to abandon them completely at this time of year. Garden centres will have plenty of hellebores in stock, along with other winter-dependable perennials.

Liriope muscari and *L. spicata*

These are clump-forming perennials. Some cultivars have leaves so dark they are practically black. They are good candidates for grouping with other plants in interesting combinations. Good for ground cover or edging beside a path.

Hellebores

The *Helleborus* genus has tons of choices that are hardy. The Christmas rose is popular for its midwinter white flowers, often appearing in the snow. Others have flowers in shades of green, red and purple. Wonderful for winter interest, it has great foliage too.

Arum italicum (Italian lords-and-ladies)

A tuberous perennial with broad arrow-shaped leaves that appear in the autumn, it grows to 30 centimetres. The foliage dies back in the summer just as the berries appear, which we feel are underwhelming. After the berries die, the foliage reappears, remaining until the next summer, and is lush and green all winter.

Acorus gramineus (sweet flag)

Everyone thinks this is a grass, but it's actually an evergreen perennial. Native to Japan, it has soft, curved leaves and it is grown mainly for this sweet-smelling foliage. In the winter, it has beautiful texture and pleasing green, white and chartreuse colours. It will also grow in a damp spot.

Iris unguicularis (Algerian iris)

Strap-like evergreen foliage and lilac flowers from October to March.

Viola tricolor

This produces neat flowers with 'faces' in shades of yellow, blue, violet and white. It flowers in autumn and often in winter and self-seeds readily.

Bergenia

There are several species/cultivars that bear pink or white flowers from January to April.

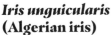

Carex

Texture can be hard to come by in a leafless winter border. If you need to brighten up the garden on a dark winter day, the colourful variegated foliage of *Carex oshimensis* 'Evergold' or *C. morrowii* 'Variegata' are hard to beat.

Carex comans

'Bronze Perfection' is a fabulous evergreen sedge with a naturally cascading habit that adds colour and movement to drab borders. These reliable grasses are neat and compact, making them perfect for winter patio containers. Combine them with some bright winter pansies for a long-lasting, colourful display.

Paul's plant of the month

Galanthus 'Mrs McNamara'

I love snowdrops too much not to mention them. There are literally thousands of varieties of these wonderful spring bulbs, but a few are particularly useful. For me in County Carlow, 'Mrs McNamara' is without fail in flower by Christmas Day. By mid-January it's all over, but by then other main season snowdrops begin to take centre stage. To have a plant in flower that early is invaluable, especially at a time where the garden looks so grey. Plant them in the green or when they have foliage on for maximum success.

Fruit-tree pruning

PAUL

Too much pruning in one season can stress a tree, so if you think a lot of work is required – for example if you are renovating an overgrown tree – plan to do the work over a few years. I learned this lesson the hard way rejuvenating trees that took years to properly produce fruit again after a severe butchering! An annual prune will help to ensure that fruit trees remain healthy and, weather permitting, produce good crops next year.

As we are in the depths of winter – the dormant period from November to bud-burst in early March – it's pruning time for apples and pears (unless they are trained as espaliers, fans or cordons, which are pruned in summer). Don't prune the stone fruits, such as plums, almonds and cherries, as they are susceptible to silver leaf disease if pruned in winter.

Why do we prune fruit trees? The reasons are twofold: to develop and maintain a strong framework; and to encourage blossoming and fruiting. A strong framework of branches is required to support fruit that at cropping time can be very heavy and snap weaker branches in two. Ideally you want an open canopy that you can see through, allowing good air circulation, which is important for disease prevention. As well as this, you need sunlight to be able to penetrate to all of the tree to allow for fruit ripening.

Remember all the Ds as you begin the process of pruning. Removing dead, diseased and damaged material should always be your first step, regardless of what it is you're pruning. So, armed with a clean pair of secateurs and loppers or a small saw, go out to the garden and take a good look at the tree before you dive in. Examine the overall shape. If it's getting too big for the space, you might need to cut back some of the top growth – a telescopic loppers can reach higher branches. Remove any suckers and any water shoots (straight little stems that pop up vertically on branches) as these are non-productive. You will often find branches crossing each other or rubbing against each other – these should be removed as they can lead to disease. Anything that has died or looks rotten should also be completely removed. And judiciously remove branches where necessary to open up the shape of the tree and allow light and air in.

If your tree is a spur-bearing variety, i.e. bears fruit on small stubby side shoots, and most of the apples and pears we grow are, cut back the previous year's growth on all the main branches by about a third to an outward facing bud, and shorten any side shoots (laterals) to just above five buds. Tip-bearing varieties form fruit at the tip of the laterals, so they require a lighter touch – leave alone any laterals that are around 30 centimetres in length. More vigorous side shoots can be lightly pruned back to just above a bud to encourage more tips to form.

Frequently Asked Questions

Throughout a year of doing nightly broadcasts we have found ourselves answering the same questions over and over! While we love the fact that there are so many new gardeners and are hugely excited by their enthusiasm, we thought we might address the questions that crop up again and again.

When do I prune my hydrangea?

Our favourite question: if we had a euro for every hydrangea-related question, we could build our own Versailles.

Broadly speaking, there are two different types of hydrangea and they need treating slightly differently.

The old-fashioned hydrangea that everyone's granny grew in her garden and that comes in pinks and blues is *Hydrangea macrophylla*. They flower on growth made in the previous season, so if you prune them in spring you'll lose all the flowers. The trick here is to thin out the oldest stems and allow new ones to take their place. Leave some of last year's growth to ensure that you get flowers this year.

The other types are *H. paniculata* and *H. arborescens*, 'Limelight' and 'Annabelle' being the two most commonly grown of each respectively. They tend to have white to lime-green or soft pink flowers. They flower on growth made in this growing season, so they can be pruned as much or as little as you like. Ideally prune to the same framework every year once they are established.

How do I get rid of moss on my lawn?

Why do you want to? We love moss and actively encourage it. It slows the grass down and is soft underfoot. We would be happy to leave it be, as it's often a result of compacted soil and poor light, which are problems we can't always easily deal with in the garden. However, we do understand that people love their lawns. As a result this is probably the most frequently asked gardening question of all time.

The reason you have moss in your lawn? There's no black and white answer. Let's go to the root of the problem. Moss loves the climate of these islands, damp and often wet. Couple that with some shade and you have moss nirvana. So first try to address these problems. If the area gets wet often, consider drainage. If it's very dark, maybe you need to allow more light in. Even if you have perfect conditions, you'll still get moss because we tend to cut our lawns to the same level all the time and they shed bits of dead leaves occasionally, creating shade for moss to thrive in.

You can kill moss with a range of products. We don't favour using chemicals, so go for organic alternatives where possible. Sulphate of iron is effective at killing the moss, but that's only part of the problem. Once the moss is dead and blackened you need to remove it. Use a strong leaf rake and heavily rake the moss and the dead thatch. The lawn will look terrible for a while, but if you do this in April, as the lawn begins to grow it soon recovers.

What is the best way of keeping aphids at bay?

Aphids can cause real problems when growth begins in spring, sucking sap and often overwhelming plants. They reproduce incredibly fast. Lots of products available will kill them, but as we prefer to garden organically, the best way we've found to control them is by spraying infected plants with soapy water. Simply put a few drops of washing-up liquid in a spray container and then fill with water. Give this a good shake and spray directly onto infected leaves. If the infestation is heavy it may be an idea to spray the plant with a hose first to knock off the worst of the aphids

Is weed membrane any good?

There is no doubt that it's effective, and in certain situations it can be useful. However, as a rule we don't use it, for a variety of reasons. It tends to trap moisture and air and the soil below it often becomes stale. It doesn't help the earthworm population and it's a real pain to plant into. Once the mulch layer you place on top degrades or gets old the membrane is exposed, which isn't the most attractive thing. We would recommend using it for

paths and large areas of weeds you need to control, such as in a vegetable garden.

How do I hide my septic tank?

This is an issue unique to those of us who are lucky enough to live in the countryside. Septic tanks deal with waste, but often the service point is an above-ground slab of concrete or plastic, and usually it's plonked in the middle of a lawn. The best way to disguise anything like this is with more planting. We like to use ground-cover plants that will carpet the ground and grow in the often poor, shallow soil that is used to fill around these tanks. *Ceanothus thyrsiflorus* var. *repens,* or creeping Californian lilac is a favourite and has the added advantage of being evergreen. *Persicaria affinis* 'Darjeeling Red' is another great plant to carpet shallow soil. *Geranium* 'Rozanne' is a fantastic ground-cover plant, but any hardy geranium would work.

What vegetable is the easiest to grow?

This is a difficult one as most vegetables are relatively easy, though there are a few exceptions. The only thing we would hesitate to suggest a beginner grows is asparagus, as it takes years to crop properly and is an investment in the garden. Our preferred answer to this question is grow whatever veg you like. It's so important to only grow what you know you will eat. We have a saying that no good story starts with a salad, so we would never grow salad leaves, despite them being easy. Radishes are another classic – they're easy to grow, but they divide opinion. There's no point having an abundance of a crop you don't want!

Why has my wisteria not flowered?

Another favourite question. The answer is an unusual one and there isn't usually a quick fix. Most wisteria these days are grafted, so they flower sooner than wisteria grown from seed, which can take eight years and more to flower. To ensure you get a plant that will flower, the best advice is to buy them in full bloom. That way you know the plant has begun flowering and should flower every year thereafter. It may not flower the year immediately after planting, especially if it suffers shock in the first year after being planted. Improving the soil and regular watering should help reduce shock.

Why have my daffodils got leaves but no flowers?

This is a very common problem, often referred to as daffodil blindness. It is simply when your daffodils come up, very healthily, in spring with lots of lush leaves and few or small flowers. The most likely reason is that they have become congested, which means that they don't have enough room to form a good-sized bulb. So dig them up, take them apart and replant them. Then allow foliage to die back naturally to replenish the bulb. The best time to do this is anytime from March to May, when the leaves are still visible

Something is eating my cabbage plants ... help!

This is likely one of two things. Cabbage and its relatives are delicious to slugs and snails and are often the first plants to be attacked and often stripped. Beer traps and nightly patrols are both options for controlling them organically. You can get organic slug pellets, but we do try to avoid using them outside at all costs as birds, hedgehogs and other animals may still ingest them.

The other culprit is the caterpillar of the cabbage white butterfly. On summer days you often see these bright white butterflies around cabbage plants, but beware – they are about to lay their eggs. When the caterpillars hatch they feast on the leaves. A good net over the cabbages is the best way to keep the butterflies off your precious crop

Why are plants grafted?

In essence, the reason for grafting is to produce a top-quality plant. Plants are like humans; they have their strengths and weaknesses. Some are very vigorous, tolerant of drought and disease, but lack other qualities, like flowers. Diarmuid and Paul could be used as examples. Diarmuid's strength is garden design; Paul's is the craft and cultivation of plants. So we perform best when we combine our talents to create something magic.

Looking at plants, let's take apples as an example. Some of the best-known and most delicious varieties of apple make weak trees in their own right, but they produce good fruit. They are often weak and prone to problems. Another problem is that they are just too big, meaning that they will outgrow a space if grown on their own root.

The answer is to graft the better variety onto the root of a strong growing apple. When it comes to apples there are a lot of commonly commercially used rootstocks, all with slightly different characteristics, and all suited to different sites. M9 apple rootstocks are the most commonly used ones in a garden as they are dwarfing, meaning the tree won't outgrow a small garden. If you're putting a fruit tree in a pot, M667 are ultra-dwarfing and are the best choice – they are often sold as patio apples. By picking the correct rootstock, you'll be able to grow more varieties and keep them healthier.

Other plants are grafted so that they flower sooner (wisteria) and others because they are slow or difficult to root (Acers). The most important point to note is that all grafts are clones of each other.

Why is my plum tree not fruiting?

Plums and a lot of fruit trees often have off years. Older varieties tended to have glut years followed by a year or sometimes even two with little or no fruit. So patience is the first bit of advice. Choosing a good reliable variety is the other key point. The final thing that may be causing the problem is a late frost when the blooms are out. This destroys the flowers before they get a chance to be pollinated so they can set fruit.

How can I keep my plants flowering for longer?

Everyone wants to have a kaleidoscope of colour in their garden for as long as possible. When a plant is blooming the best way to ensure the maximum number of flowers is to continually deadhead the plant. This is particularly true for annuals such as cosmos and sweet peas. Just snip off any spent flowers to allow the energy to go back into the plant instead of producing seed. A good feed will help plants flower too. Tomato feed is high in potash and is a great quick feed if you want a plant to produce lots of blooms.

Can I leave the soil bare in winter?

Ideally, no. It's sometimes difficult in the vegetable garden, but we would always try to have a cover on the soil, either a living one or mulch. A living cover could be something like a green manure, which is a crop that is grown to be dug back into the soil to help improve it. Often they will germinate quickly in autumn and allow the soil to have something growing in it all winter. Mulches will help retain moisture and help to reduce leaching, which is a problem when soil is exposed over winter.

I have a camellia which is in full bloom at the moment but I notice there's lots of black stuff on all the leaves. Should I prune it?

No, there's no need to cut or prune your camellias. The foliage is suffering from a common problem – sooty mould. This is a fungus that grows on the excretions of aphids and scale insects. You can clean the mould off with water but really you want to prevent the pests that are feeding on your camellia. Cushion scale insects are often the culprit – check the undersides of the leaves to see if there are any eggs or insects. You can spray in June to break the cycle of these little pests – organic sprays are available if you don't like using chemicals.

What plants can I grow in dry shade?

People come to us with this all the time. Most people shudder at the mention of dry shade, but there are actually plants that will do well here and once established can be left to their own devices. The most important thing is to water them in year one as they establish. *Dryopteris* ferns, hellebores, *Cyclamen hederifolium*, *Anemone japonica*, astrantias, lily of the valley, *Liriope muscari*, snowdrops, wood anemone, *Geranium macrorrhizum* and epimediums are all plants that, once established, will cope with dry shade.

I want to grow potatoes in pots; what soil do you recommend?

Use a multipurpose peat-free compost mixed with some garden soil if you have it or some loam-based compost from the garden centre. Add farmyard manure as well – they're heavy feeders, so the richer the soil the better.

Opposite: Japanese anemone (*Anemone japonica*) grows well in dry shade.

Acknowledgements

We'd like to thank all the team at Gill books, especially Sarah Liddy, Aoibheann Molumby, Laura King, Claire O'Flynn and Teresa Daly.

The idea for this book emerged through our broadcasts on Instagram during lockdown. A community of like-minded gardeners, affectionately known as the riff-raff, came together to share information and enjoy cheesy music and irreverent humour. Thank you to you all for your endurance!

Paul: I'd like to thank those who have encouraged, coaxed, cajoled and taken leaps of faith with me: to Angela, who, in her life, inspired me and pushed me forward; to Cara, for being that force in the early days; and to Sue, Bleddyn and all those who have helped to further my knowledge of and joy for plants. Finally, to my family and friends for their support and their advice, which I might not always heed but do appreciate – thank you.

Index

Photographs are indicated by page numbers in bold type. Occasionally, the same page number will appear twice; this is to indicate that there is information in the text relating to the photograph.